I0815528

FUTURE NEEDS WISDOM

FUTURE NEEDS WISDOM

AN INTELLECTUAL MEMOIR

HELGA NOWOTNY

The Chinese University of Hong Kong Press

Future Needs Wisdom: An Intellectual Memoir
By Helga Nowotny

ISBN: 978-988-237-320-4

The Chinese University of Hong Kong Press
The Chinese University of Hong Kong
Sha Tin, N.T., Hong Kong
Fax: +852 2603 7355
Email: cup@cuhk.edu.hk
Website: cup.cuhk.edu.hk

Printed in Hong Kong

"Future Needs Wisdom" is the last line of a haiku written by Helga Nowotny:

Human company
Invisible algorithms
Future needs wisdom

TABLE OF CONTENTS

ACKNOWLEDGEMENTS

"I would like to thank my wife" is the tongue-in-cheek title of an "acknowledgements of acknowledgements" by Sarah Lonsdale, in which she reflects on the attraction this burgeoning new literary genre exerts. New, because it never used to be like this. She follows the literary critic Terry Caesar who surmises that the spawning of ever larger and more complex acknowledgements is a byproduct of feminism. Male authors are beginning to realize that while they heroically struggled with their writing, their wives, partners, or children were carrying the burdens of everyday chores. But this alone cannot explain the rise of acknowledgments that have become an obligatory feature in the performance of personhood. With more women academics writing books, Londsdale believes, a more collegiate and collaborative mood entered the acknowledgement sections, rendering them more autobiographical and personal and, paradoxically, thereby confirming the stereotype of women as more caring (Londsdale 2023).

Acknowledgements certainly have become more copious, opening a door to let the reader glimpse an otherwise hidden part of the life of the author and the making of the text. Tidbits of exotic revelations may be added, intended to add color to what appears otherwise the sober product of the author's laborious efforts. Acknowledgements then engage in playful collusion with the reader's curiosity, even nosiness, born from the wish to know more about the author's life and the circumstances of writing. Disclosure can cover a wide range, from the fabulous places and treats enjoyed by the author to tragic events that unfolded during the process of the book's gestation. One feature stands out however: the list of names in the acknowledgments continues to grow. It not only includes, as one would expect, friends and colleagues, but the networks of friends, colleagues, students, and others, displaying the author's status in the academic world. I wonder whether this has not, especially in the US academic context, become the way to reduce the risk of negative reviews by those who are profusely thanked to have contributed with their ideas to the product they may be asked to review. But regardless of the motivation and however witty, graceful or original the content and style of the acknowledgement, the fact remains that each product incorporates and is based on the labor of others who contribute in a variety of ways to its making, including what feminists once called "emotional labor."

This poses a double quandary for an intellectual memoir. I can either enter the competition and join efforts to be even more inclusive and extravagant. Or, my list becomes even longer, as it covers an extended stretch of my life, different contexts in which I move and the multiple dimensions that are covered. In my apartment in Vienna, I have a wall in one corridor covered with the badges I brought back from the many conferences and meetings I have attended. In numerous of these occasions, I have met people from whom I learned something and whose ideas might have had some influence on me. I feel it would be ludicrous and simply impossible to name all those who have helped me in ways often unknown to them along my long trajectory. There are also those more intimate and rare occasions, when I set down with someone or in a small group, where a real, deep conversation developed which all of us felt rewarding. Such encounters can take place not only in the proverbial bar, but anywhere. Even if hard pressed, it would be difficult to dig them up from memory, yet I am sure that they too, provide an important source in the origin and circulation of ideas.

The only possibility left to me is therefore to express my profound apologies for not explicitly naming and thanking all those whom I sincerely would like to thank. I am aware of and grateful for the support I have received from many sides and the free-floating exchange of ideas with colleagues and friends in many places around the world on different occasions. Nor can I thank this time those who offered me the luxury of a nice place where I could write in quiet comfort, as the delivery of the manuscript had to meet a deadline.

This brings me to those who initiated and accompanied the process of publication. Winifred Sin and Ye Minlei from The Chinese University of Hong Kong Press came up with the idea to write a book about myself and my work. I had never considered to do so and was very reluctant to accept. Yet, Winifred persisted and persuaded me to proceed. Initially, I only wanted to expand the interview with Elena, but when I sat down to write, my recollection and reflection began to flow. The problem was to carve out sufficient time for writing despite a busy schedule, which reminded me briefly of the period described later as living a double life. My long-term personal assistant, Barbara Grassauer, did everything she could in many ingenious ways to shield me efficiently from outside interference. As usual, she also thoughtfully took care of the formal requirements of the manuscript and helped me in the selection of the photographs included. Many thanks to Winifred and Minlei for taking the initiative, without which this book would not exist, and to Barbara for helping me to bring it into existence.

I asked three persons, dear and near to me, to read and comment as the work progressed. My granddaughter Isabel Frey, who assisted me when writing my last book, had to decline, as she was engaged in finishing her Ph.D. at the University of Music and Performing Arts Vienna with a deadline looming also for her. This did not keep her from continuing her political engagement in the form of co-organizing several "Standing Together" events for the Israeli and Palestinian victims in the war between Israel and Hamas. She also continued to perform Yiddish songs with her beautiful voice in concerts, one of which I was able to attend.

I also turned to my friend Alexander Polzin, whose sculptures and other artistic works have accompanied and inspired me in unforeseen ways over many years. The sculptures speak to me through the ways in which they absorb and shape the space around them, turning it inward and then again outward to radiate and change the environment in which they find their place. Alexander is extremely well read and knowledgeable in many fields. It is with great modesty that he brings what he knows and what drives him into every conversation. I have come to treasure and trust his artistic sensibilities and literary judgement and Alexander encouraged me to proceed. He pleaded with me to explain in greater depth what I believed was obvious. I am grateful for our long friendship and look forward to more of it.

Carlo Rizzuto accompanied me also this time when writing the memoir. We often joke about our different approaches to discarding things. For him, as an experimental physicist who built his first radio when he was fourteen, nothing is to be thrown away as it might still be useful in the future and will be repurposed, while I feel liberated if I can leave behind what I think is no longer needed. Writing a memoir has obliged me to retrace parts of my past and to retrieve encounters, events, and ideas that I had already forgotten or consigned to the bin of my thoughts. Thus, I came to realize the traces they have left, which confirmed their usefulness, although in unexpected ways. My thanks go to Carlo for being able to laugh together, the pure joy of being together, and everything else it entails.

Vienna, Spring 2024

PREFACE

An Interview with Myself

The idea of writing an intellectual memoir never occurred to me. Yet here it is. It started with a long, in-depth interview. There is nothing unusual about it, except that it took place on a splendid summer afternoon. The sun was still high, but the heat started to retreat. From the terrace one could see the beach crowded with the typical mix of people; those who would soon get up to catch the train bringing them back into their urban habitat, and those who would later meet their friends for an aperitivo or host them for dinner in their summer house. Beyond the beach was the sea—one of the innumerable beautiful coastlines of the Mediterranean, shaped by the waves gently caressing the stones, sand, and rocks, just as they had done during the summer months for thousands of years.

My guest and I also had an appointment for a dinner later in the evening. Before, we engaged in what we had planned some time ago: a long interview to appear in the journal *Sociologica*, "Helga Nowotny in Conversation with Elena Esposito" (Esposito 2019). We spoke about my work and life, my scientific biography, the role of technologies in the ways we experience time, the organization and funding of science at EU level, the ongoing transformation of the research system, and we touched on gender issues—aptly summarized in the abstract that precedes the published interview. I had known Elena for some time, and we had planned to meet when she was a Fellow at the Wissenschaftskolleg zu Berlin, WIKO (see p.16), the most prestigious Institute for Advanced Study in Europe. I know the WIKO well, as I had been there in the first year of its existence, a genuine "Ur-Fellow," followed by short-term returns, and can confirm that it is unmatched in the generous academic working conditions it provides for those fortunate to spend a truly unforgettable year on its premises. But my short stay with Elena came to nothing. Like so many other events, it had to be cancelled due to the COVID-19 pandemic.

The interview with Elena lays out the grid of my scientific trajectory, and I will take the liberty to borrow amply from this source. But an intellectual memoir differs from answering questions posed by an interviewer with whom one establishes a face-to-face communicative bond. I remember many good and bad interviews. Depending on the nature and purpose, the interviewer seeks to elicit from the interviewee the information looked for. This may simply consist in obtaining a soundbite or an authoritative confirmation of what the interviewer wants to hear. An interview is intended for a specific audience which shapes content, form, and the language used. Every time, I am surprised how much the outcome depends on the personal interaction that arises in the conversation—and how unpredictable it is. With Elena it was excellent—but how different is it from writing an intellectual memoir?

This time, there is no external interviewer. Rather, I am interviewing myself. This may sound stranger than it is, but it remains a peculiar situation in which I engage in a sympathetic and deep conversation with myself—and I claim that nobody knows me better than I do—while keeping a cool, analytic distance at the same time. I strive for a good balance between my role as interviewer and as interviewee. I am guided by the sense of what may be relevant for an audience I barely know, but it also must be meaningful for me. Above all, the outcome must satisfy my criteria of internalized quality standards. If not, I have only myself to blame.

The communicative structure of an interview consists of questions and answers which shape the conversational flow and moves it forward. Questions can be good or bad; clever or stupid; mean or supportive. They can be to the point or vague and even toxic, depending on the objectives of the interview and how it is framed. In a cross-examination, interviewer and interviewee are at opposite ends by design. Another situation arises when journalists try to extract information from politicians who have been coached what not to say with many empty words. In what follows, I will try to be as honest and open with myself as possible. Inevitably there will be gaps, some imposed by space, others because I do not consider them to be relevant.

An intellectual memoir has a defined objective. It is not "a life," a biographic genre so dear to the British, and I have little to say that is not directly or indirectly related to what has been driving me to do the work I have done. An intellectual memoir seeks to dig deeper into the connections that are not obvious. It attempts to unearth guiding concepts, their origins and relations among them, why they turned out to be fruitful or obsolete. It may even aim to shed some light on the origins of these concepts and why they took on the importance they achieved. An intellectual memoir dwells on methods, instruments and working conditions, on who influenced whom, and on the intellectual and academic networks that provide support. Ideally, it should result in an intellectual portrait that brings to life the numerous contingencies that shape a life and work, from one's upbringing and early and later education to those achievements that justify the interest in a person's trajectory. In my case, it will also touch what it means to be a woman in science.

Good questions are of overall importance, but what makes a good question depends on the context. Posing a good question is an art and is surprisingly rare.[1] A good question can pry open what was closed before, render visible that was invisible, lead to a switch in perspective or discover a new angle for what had been taken for granted. It may act like a slow burning fuse, linger in the mind of the listener without having been answered, but refusing to go away. These are the questions that point to something beyond seeing the world as it is, because they carry the subversive message "it could be otherwise" (Nowotny 2000). Often, these questions contain a normative dimension. They matter, because they alert us to the many contingencies in our lives and even those of societies, while focusing attention on what might serve as a compass for navigating troubling and confusing circumstances. They widen the space of the imagination and push us to confront the relationship between what the Austrian writer Robert Musil called the "Möglichkeitsraum" and the "Wirklichkeitsraum," the space of what is possible and the space of what is real. Playing at the shifting interface between them enables creativity to emerge and innovation to occur, as scientists and artists know very well.[2]

---

1 It has become customary for the speaker in an academic conference to thank the questioner from the audience with "this is a very good question." In practice, this is only the polite acknowledgement that the question is easy to answer, offering the speaker the opportunity to confirm their brilliance.

2 According to Stuart Kauffman's Theory of the Adjacent Possible, the evolving biosphere and every existing organism create new possibilities, find new functions, and uses that cannot be predicted (Kauffman 2002). For Brian Arthur,

For research to be productive it is essential to begin with a good question. It functions like a flashlight, in search for a promising path in the darkness of the still unknown ahead. Asking a good research question gives focus to the search and although fundamental research is inherently uncertain, it provides a guiding sense of direction and stimulates the excitement to explore what is yet unknown. To find the way and to move on, curiosity, passion, and perseverance will be needed. A good research question hovers on the edge between knowledge that is already ascertained and new, emerging knowledge. It is but the beginning of what often is a long and tortuous road before this new knowledge will be validated, accepted, and turned into knowledge that is certain, although in science all certain knowledge is always only preliminary. It will be modified, superseded, expanded, incorporated, and replaced by more and better knowledge. But there is nothing like the excitement of the beginnings, of finding something that seemingly nobody had found before.

In my book *Insatiable Curiosity: Innovation in a Fragile Future*, I have explored curiosity as a trait that humans share with other organisms, although only humans have language to express it. It is not always welcome and the *libido sciendi*, the lust for knowledge, repeatedly has been forbidden or restricted by religious and secular authorities. Curiosity is one of the driving forces behind scientific activity and the arts, but often it solicits ambivalent reactions. Contemporary societies are obsessed with the "quest for innovation," which is society's response to the uncertainties that come with the acceleration of scientific-technological advances. While science and

---

the origins of evolution of technology and hence innovation are the outcome of combinatorial evolutionary processes, whereby existing parts are combined in novel ways, fusing experience and knowledge (Arthur 2009).

the arts need autonomy to flourish, many efforts are deployed to channel their creative potential in desirable and wanted directions. This is the taming of curiosity by society that generates new tensions that are difficult to resolve. Human curiosity is insatiable as especially the scientific and technological possibilities are immense, but also due to the insatiability of human wants and needs, leading to the craving for more in material, cognitive or emotional terms (Nowotny 2008).

Students working for a Master's thesis, or a Ph.D. thesis / dissertation, often have great difficulties in finding and formulating the question that drives them, and academic teachers often fail to prepare them sufficiently well to nurture their curiosity (Grossman, Jackson, and Nowotny 2020).[3] As a thesis supervisor, I had to push hard, especially my Ph.D. students, to come up with a question to which they could relate beyond having it entrusted on them from outside. If they want to follow their own path, they must learn to think for themselves, beginning with the questions "what do I want to know"? and "why do I want to know this"? Intrinsic motivation matters and so does honesty: why am I interested in this question, where does this interest come from and, perhaps even: what has it to do with me? Those wanting to pursue a career in research must learn to be persistent. Inevitably, there will be times of utter frustration. "Nature does not easily yield its secrets," as the natural philosophers put it in the early days of modern science. Great scientists in our midst today succeeded despite the odds.

---

3 Writing the Afterword for the book, I was struck by the urgent emphasis to (re)introduce the study of curiosity into the classroom and academia in the United States and to let students practice their own curiosity while guiding them to reflexively analyze where it leads. If the only goal of education is to equip students with the aspiration "to get a job," the scope is dangerously narrowed, leading to what some call the system of being broken.

They were passionate, even obstinate, and continued to pursue the questions that drove them. Yet, without the will and strength to persist, they would not have been able to achieve getting the answers nor—finally—be rewarded with the Nobel Prize.[4]

Good questions can be good enough questions. In what follows I will elicit the underlying themes, concepts and questions that undergird my research and how they hang together. My academic trajectory is marked by the contingencies of my life and blessed by the privileges that academia still holds, despite the vulnerabilities and precariousness to which the younger generation are exposed today. Not that I did not also experience periods which were full of doubt and insecurity. But I was lucky to belong to a cohort convinced that the world is open for them. We were full of confidence that in case one prospect did not work out, there were always other tempting options worth to be explored.

Today, this kind of confidence into being able to find one's future seems to have vanished in many parts of the academic world. Depending on time and place, and on the national, economic, cultural, and political context, it has been replaced by different kinds of imaginaries and projections, but also by despair, often shrouded in what has become an involuted, and sometimes tortuous search for identity, aggravated by "woke" and "anti-woke" politics (Lamont 2023). I am convinced that the confidence my generation experienced had

---

4 My favorite role models among Nobel laureates "against all odds" are Stefan W. Hell, Nobel Prize in Chemistry 2014, "for the development of super-resolved fluorescence microscopy" and Katalin Karikó, Nobel Prize in Physiology or Medicine 2023, "for … discoveries concerning nucleoside base modifications that enabled the development of effective mRNA vaccines against COVID-19." Katalin Karikó, *Breaking Through: My Life in Science* (New York: Crown, 2023) https://www.nobelprize.org/categories/speeches/

much to do with recognition. Despite our disagreements we discovered we had voice and agency. We exchanged recognition with each other, which made us eager and put trust in our perhaps too naïve belief that we can change the world.

Mine was a generation that had found its voice in the USA through opposition against the Vietnam War and in the student protest movement it unleashed which I experienced first-hand during my years at Columbia University, New York. The defense of my Ph.D. thesis could not take place at the premises of the university as the building was occupied by students. The Ph.D. committee moved to the living room in the nearby home of Paul F. Lazarsfeld, my supervisor. In Europe, the 1968 movement swept away the ultra-conservative hierarchies of the academic establishment. In Germany and Austria, it also brought with it a confrontation between the younger generation and their parents about the part they played in the countries' Nazi past. In France and Italy, it was partly the colonial past, partly other grievances that fueled the revolt against "the establishment" and hierarchies of any kind.

A good enough question implies to have a sense of direction and to select among the many existing possibilities. It has a focus but avoids premature closure. Having thus set the bar for myself, what do I expect to extract from my academic trajectory that is worth being shared and transmitted in the hope that my experience has something to offer to others? What is worth being extracted from the contingencies of my life and what can be learned from the privileges that I enjoy?

Contingencies in many forms and contexts form the "red threads" that are present in my work. Just like mutations in the biological realm, contingencies crop up also in the social world in different constellations, unexpectedly and everywhere. They find a crack in closed walls and go against the existing order. I have encountered them in such seemingly different arenas as policymaking as well as in science, where they take the form of serendipity, a powerful and welcome ally of all practitioners of research. In public policy discourse, the perception is predominantly that of decision-makers, people in official functions who decide which policy measures to adopt when confronted with challenges and to solve pressing problems. In practice, the outcome is known, but relatively little about how and why certain decisions were reached. I have been engaged in science-policy advice on numerous occasions and sufficiently well-placed to observe the processes that ultimately led to a policy to be adopted or a decision to be taken. The outcome never was straightforward. Personal contacts and relationships of likes and dislikes, being at the right place at the right time, getting attention or being ignored, all play a role.

Historians follow the contingencies that play out on a grand scale. They encounter them, for instance, when reconstructing in minute detail the unfolding of the US-Cuba missile crisis which, for the first time, brought the world to a possible nuclear brink (Stern 2012). Some eerie resemblance to today's volatile geopolitical situation emerges when rereading Barbara Tuchman's *The Guns of August* or Christopher Clark's *The Sleepwalkers,* the classical historical accounts of the processes and contingencies leading to WWI. The major events and what preceded them, the personalities involved, the interests and resources of the different parties and the shifting distribution of power are vividly described in historical detail. We are led to ponder the contingencies that are an inherent feature of every complex system. When looking at an example of our present days, we seem dangerously close to reaching the tipping point which may trigger a phase transition leading to societal collapse (Turchin 2023).

In science, contingencies arise in the form of serendipity, which manifests itself in two closely related ways. First comes an encounter with a phenomenon or finding one does not expect, which happens rather frequently. However, what follows makes all the difference: one must understand the significance of such a chance encounter. In our book on the discovery of high-temperature superconductivity and its aftermath, Ulrike Felt and I describe how only a few months before K. Alex Müller and J. Georg Bednorz made their breakthrough discovery (for which they received the Nobel Prize in 1987 in record time of one year later), a French research team using somewhat different material had made the same observation. Yet, they dismissed it as they did not recognize its significance.

According to Louis Pasteur: *le hasard ne favorise que les ésprits préparés* (chance favors only the prepared minds), but can preparedness be planned and if so, how? For us, Müller and Bednorz's discovery highlights the interface between their individual drive which led them to conduct their research systematically, obtaining in the end what they were looking for, and the social organization of science. Which conditions are conducive for creativity and what can be done to prepare a scientific mind? An innovative breakthrough escapes predictability by definition. There is an inherent tension between the social organization of scientific research, which is set up as a stable framework for reasonable expectations and predictable, reproducible results, and the unexpected, unpredictable discovery (Nowotny and Felt 1997).

Contingency is closely related to the other theme that pervades much of my work—uncertainty—and what I call the cunning of uncertainty (Nowotny 2015). The more we acknowledge uncertainty, the less threatened we feel by it. I show how uncertainty is interwoven into human existence, but also how fundamental research thrives at the cusp of uncertainty. It is an integral part of the creative process, in the sciences and the arts. It is part of innovation as every decision taken may result in unintended consequences. The key question how to cope with uncertainty was catapulted on the public stage during the COVID-19 pandemic. While many people were craving for certainty which made them retreat further in fear or aggressive behavior and politicians engaged in opportunistic simplifications and false promises, science exemplified how to face up to uncertainty. Scientists showed how to make the most of it by relentlessly pushing forward. Admittedly, communication with the public was difficult and much went awry. Yet, there is a lot to be learned from science and, as societies will be confronted with even greater uncertainty ahead, acquiring a better understanding of it and remaining open towards a future that evolves will be essential.

I have no theory of contingency to offer but am convinced that the threads and concepts that are interwoven in my work, and in writing reflexively about them, do hang together. Mine is a plea to keep the future open and acknowledge the uncertainty that is inherent in it and pervades our lives. I follow the dialectics between the wish to know the future and hence to strive for as much predictability as one can possibly achieve and the encounter with the unpredictable. There is the deeply rooted anxiety to be and remain in control which is always at risk to be undermined by the illusion of control as well as the opening of the human imagination through insatiable curiosity and the reaction by society that seeks to channel it and tame curiosity. The lens I use is that of science and technology studies, which enables me to follow in concrete and empirical ways how science and technology reveal the dynamics of these processes, generate, and drive them. However, the "solutions" science and technology have to offer must never be reduced to mere "technological fixes" or narrowed to a "techno-solutionism," as this will only displace the underlying contradictions and conflicts, leading to new problems.

On a practical as well as on a theoretical level, I want to know how change happens in society. There is much official political rhetoric, and even political will, about transformation towards greater sustainability, but very little is known about the mechanisms and how they work. We can describe many processes of change in retrospect but have to rely on abstract agent-based simulation models to get a glimpse of what might happen next. I hear politicians speak about "managing sustainable transition" and bold claims by academics about a "transition science." When I see graphs with boxes carrying labels of abstract concepts and arrows standing for imagined feedbacks, it reminds me of the bygone age of modernity founded on the belief that everything can be planned, streamlined, measured, monitored, and controlled. Deep down, I am convinced that this is not the case, but I am challenged to come up with an alternative way of explaining change.

Much has been written about the hubris of modernity. Its achievements have been celebrated (Pinker 2018) and the horrific outcomes of the "intentions to do good" in the 20th century have painstakingly been described (Scott 1998). Today, we are confronted with the fallout of what had been excluded from the planning, as the degradation of the natural environment and its consequences pile up before our eyes. Even the idea of the future lost its previous attractiveness and fascination as the present fills with microplastics and other debris of consumption and an overload of information. The acceleration of technological change leaves us too little time to think and no free space to experiment with ways that lead to greater benefits for all. The future engulfs the present and it seems that we have lost our temporal bearings—a theme to which I will return.

These are some of the reasons why we should treasure contingencies and embrace uncertainty. Instead of clinging to obsolete dichotomies invented during modernity to ward off the fear of social, political, and cultural disorder, we should welcome ambivalence. We live at a time when we are faced with the messiness of the social world, unleashed by scientific ingenuity, technological progress, political hubris, and human folly. We face a dilemma that is well known. We can try to get back on track, whatever it means and whatever it takes through reform, restructuring and reimagining the future. Or we can boldly strike out in new directions, carried by the conviction that the future is open and remains uncertain.

An intellectual memoir can only provide a brief, and moreover a highly subjective glimpse into my professional life, interspersed with a few anecdotes. It seems appropriate to add some scientific articles and excerpts from books I have published over the years. I hope that they offer the reader insights into the themes that have preoccupied me in my professional work and life, themes which I feel are still relevant today.

PART ONE

Regarding the future

it is important to know the past

but equally important

to be able

to leave it behind

I.

My Non-linear Academic Trajectory

Trajectories are imagined as well as performed. Imagined, in the sense that they conjure a desirable future; performed when life moves us forward on a path that most likely differs from what we imagined. In retrospect, we can account for many of the unplanned incidents, personal encounters, and factors that may have influenced the traceable path that has emerged. Maybe this is what Kierkegaard meant when he wrote that we live forwards, but we try to understand life backwards. In academia, institutions converge to design the trajectories to be taken. They pride themselves that their assessment is based on rigorous, quantitative measurements, and peer-review. Selective screening and evaluation are in line with past outcomes and preset entry bars for the next round, yet the power of selection remains in the hands of those who select.

Also, in academia a career trajectory is a course in time and unfolds over time and thus follows the time regimes that have been inscribed in it (Felt 2021). This includes formal and informal deadlines and cut-off points in terms of the lifetime of individual researchers. Prescriptive timelines, formal and informal norms privilege some and exclude others. In academic life, the ultimate goal for many remains a tenured professorship which comes with the status of being an established scientist. The entrepreneurial world had coined the term "valley of death" that awaits the numerous start-ups. Something similar exists in academia, as every postdoc knows and only few make it to the other side.

My academic trajectory started at a time when universities in Europe still followed the largely inward-looking and slow pace of elite institutions whose place in society was assured. The logic of efficiency, manifest in university rankings and in the pressure to accelerate the production by publishing in highly ranked journals, was unknown in the "World of Yesterday" so vividly captured by the great Austrian writer Stefan Zweig (Zweig 1942). For the most part, universities were in the hands of a small, conservative group of old men who acted as gatekeepers to admit into their ranks only those who they deemed worthy, meaning those resembling them. The observation that a university professor's goal in life was to "reproduce" himself in his students and assistants can already be found in Max Weber's last lecture which he delivered in 1919 at the University of Vienna (Weber 1919).

My Years at the University of Vienna

My academic career was definitely non-linear. It had its unexpected swerves, was highly uneven and certainly not planned this way. Being a good student and always having received much support from my parents, there was never a doubt that I would go to university. The choice of study was more difficult. Some of my friends were already at university, so I asked them to take me with them to "sample" courses in medicine, chemistry, biology, and sociology. The chosen method turned out to be a heuristic of elimination, and in the end I settled for law as leaving many options open for the future. At the time, its comprehensive curriculum included economics, statistics and what later became political science. I finished my doctorate in jurisprudence in record time and shortly afterwards applied for a vacant position as assistant professor in criminal law and criminology. The circumstances are worth being retold. In those days, the recruitment decision was taken by *Herr Professor* alone. As I had attended his seminars, he knew me and told me right away that it was not his intention to hire a woman. I was somewhat taken aback and asked for the reason, and he explained that his investment in me would eventually be lost, as I would get married and leave. It would have been ludicrous to insist that I would not get married, but I challenged him on grounds of merits. If he would find a man more qualified than me, he should hire him. It honors him that he accepted, and this is how I got my first job at the University of Vienna.

During the three years I spent at the Institute of Criminology I learned a lot. Foremost, about the inner workings of the judiciary system, its contradictions and the gaps between the formal norms upheld by the law and the actual practice by the different actors involved. My professor was internationally well known and highly esteemed. In many ways, he was at the forefront of the forensic and empirical side of criminology. He used methods from the natural sciences to investigate suspected crimes like insurance fraud, but we also conducted an empirical study on differences in sentencing for the same offenses in the various courts of the country. In identifying the judges who were most harsh or lenient I could put to good use what I had learned in statistics during my study.

My professor was also innovative in his teaching. Each semester he planned an excursion with his students to a penitentiary, interviewing one or two selected inmates with their back to the students, so that they could follow live. It was my task to prepare these visits by closely reading every single document that had been written about the inmate, beginning with the police records, the various stages leading up to the trial and sentence, recourse and, very important, the assessments produced by psychiatric and other experts. At times, I felt reading a novel by Dostoevsky, piecing together the socio- and psychogram of a convicted murderer, trying to understand what made the person commit the crime. I was appalled by what I called the "irresponsible cold gaze" of the psychiatric experts whose assessments were often decisive for the sentence, as judges tended to rely on them. The authority they assumed was clad in the aura of "scientific objectivity," but it was obvious to me that they mainly followed their superficial, formulaic, and openly displayed prejudices. Much later I learned that one prominent and frequently called upon expert had been intricately involved in some of the horrific euthanasia experiments conducted under the Nazi regime. He had succeeded to be reinstalled as a professor and psychiatric expert.

I also learned how to keep to the prescribed time when lecturing. Whenever my professor was on an official mission, he asked me to step in and deliver the lecture in his place. I did not need much preparation content-wise and he handed me the box of slides containing the photographed paragraphs of the criminal code he had prepared for each lecture. All I had to do was to insert them into the projector and explain what students could see on a big screen, just like a power point presentation today. The lecture was held in the large auditorium of the University of Vienna. I was barely twenty-two years young and had to speak in front of more than 200, overwhelmingly male and older students, making them listen to me attentively. I succeeded, but at least in the beginning, I was terrified to keep exactly the forty-five minutes to go through all the slides. If I went too fast, how would I fill the time after the last slide? If I was too slow, I would have to admit that I had not succeeded to cover all the slides I was supposed to present. It taught me how to keep time whenever speaking in front of an audience, but I also discovered how rare this is.

My Years at Columbia University, New York

In the end, my professor had been correct with his prediction when he recruited me, in line with what economists had claimed all along. I got married and moved with my husband to New York. My professor's investment was a loss for him, but a gain for me and, I hope, for whatever I was able to give back later. In New York, it became clear that I could not pursue my career in criminology and penal law. The next institute comparable to the one in Vienna was in Philadelphia. Overnight, I decided to enroll in a Ph.D. program in sociology at Columbia University and the next day I went to see Paul F. Lazarsfeld, a born Viennese who had left Austria before the Nazi takeover. I was eager to learn the latest methodology in sociology and he was the world-renowned founder of empirical social science research. Generously, he accepted me on a fast track, as I already had some publications to show, even though I considered myself a beginner.

During my years at Columbia University, I got an optimal introduction to sociology. Paul F. Lazarsfeld and Robert K. Merton were considered the "twin stars," representing the best of empirical methods and theory in sociology at the time. I was impressed how each of them included their students into their work and thinking, sharing the questions that preoccupied them and leading by example in moving beyond disciplinary boundaries by challenging established dogmas. Once Paul invited a guest speaker for a seminar on the work of Ervin Goffman and ethno-methodology. Paul was the uncontested leader in survey research, yet he wanted us to familiarize ourselves with what some considered a rival research program. I remember how surprised we were when he concluded by saying that he foresaw that the "soft" qualitative approach of ethnomethodology could outlive the kind of survey research that he had championed.

Robert K. Merton's lectures were an intellectual treat, presented in an optimal and carefully orchestrated way. In one of his courses, he introduced us to "Karl Marx, the sociologist," showing us the strengths and weaknesses of Marx' work. He alerted us very early to a recently published book on *The Structure of Scientific Revolutions* by Thomas Kuhn and why it was important to know about paradigm changes. Merton kindled my first interest in the sociology of science, but I was still too much rooted in my legal past to consider switching. I was fascinated by reading Max Weber anew in English—I had read some of his work in German as part of my studies in law—only to find out how much the translation differed from what he had written in German. Translations are treacherous, as is well known. Especially in science, the translated version can easily be absorbed into the dominant way of thinking or, speaking with Kuhn, into the dominant paradigm.

The years at Columbia University were also the years of the anti-Vietnam protest movement which swept across campus. The *Zeitgeist* might have contributed to me seeing the limitations of survey research as the most adequate tool to understand what happens in society and to diagnose impending changes. In an article I published in the *Graduate Student Journal*, I compared the writings of Karl Marx and Lorenz von Stein, who both happened to be in Paris in the early 1840s and witnessed the same events. For young Marx the focus was on class struggle and the role of the bourgeoisie, while von Stein, who later became a professor of political economy at the University of Vienna, viewed them as the formation of social movements and the forging of political links between proletariat and the State. As a Hegelian, the State was above society. I was fascinated by the divergence in the interpretations of the Paris uprisings as seen by these two men. The result that empirical evidence can be used and interpreted in completely different ways, depending on theoretical assumptions, the selection of different units of analysis and what counts as evidence, became the empirical material for my Ph.D. thesis, which dealt with societal changes at the macrolevel. It marked a switch from the microlevel of survey research towards larger units of analysis and their dynamics. At the time, I was only dimly aware that one of the most glaring problems for the social sciences is the gap in the analysis and methodological tools between the microlevel and the macrolevel. It remains unresolved until this day.

In the early 1970s I returned to Vienna, together with my husband and our daughter. I took up a position as Head of Department of Sociology in the Institute for Advanced Study, founded by Paul F. Lazarsfeld and Okcar Morgenstern five years earlier. The Institute for Advanced Studies Vienna (IHS) was intended to challenge Austrian universities, offering an innovative curriculum in advanced quantitative methods in economics, sociology, political science, and informatics as well as immersion in empirical projects. It hosted an illustrious group of international visiting professors, mostly from prestigious US universities, among them Nobel laureates in economics. After the period of initial funding by the Ford Foundation, it was expected that Austrian funding should take over (Huber and König 2023).

In those days, Austrian politics was dominated by *Proporz.*[1] Practically all public funding and most public positions were divided

1 Editor's note: *Proporz* is an abbreviation for "proportionality," a practice in Austria in which positions in government are distributed between political parties in a manner proportional to their electoral or public support.

between the two major political parties, who formed a series of coalition governments. This applied also to obtain funding for research projects from ministries which followed the same logic, and which partly fell upon me. When a new cohort of fellows ("Scholaren") entered the IHS, they were eager to follow the revolutionary fervor which had reached the University of Vienna with some delay. As Head of Department, I felt increasingly squeezed between the demands of the fellows to change not only the curriculum but the world, and the directorate, which was also composed in *Proporz*-like way. The days, and parts of the night, were filled with endless meetings with little or no time left for research, let alone for my private life. I needed a break and applied at the British Council for a sabbatical in Cambridge, which I obtained.

King's College, Cambridge: Half a Year of Wild Thinking

Sabbaticals are a time-honored ritual in academic life, perceived as an entitlement to break the routines of teaching and administration, with the sole purpose to devote oneself to research. Cambridge seemed to me an ideal location, given the intensity of intellectual life at its colleges. King's College granted me the status of a visiting scholar. I had access to the library and a select number of events at King's, but no other obligation. These minimal conditions fulfilled the promise of a sabbatical: having time to read and think. It became an extremely fertile period of my life, with lasting effect.

Anthony Giddens, who was not yet the well-known sociologist and prolific author he later became, was already at King's and asked me whether I would accept to be a tutor. He needed someone for a course on "The Sociology of Science, Knowledge and Belief" and as there was nobody around with a Ph.D. in sociology, I was the ideal person.

Sociology of science was equated with Robert K. Merton and thus my intellectual home ground. Sociology of knowledge as represented in the reading list turned out to be an interesting mix of the latest, and quite good, British scholarship on education and learning, including the privileges that were transmitted or withheld, and the kind of reforms needed. The last, sociology of belief, was pure anthropology, and I absorbed it with fascination. Whoever had designed the course was to be congratulated. I met my students, always two of them, in regular intervals and we discussed the assigned reading material. I found it an excellent way of teaching, alas, reserved for the privileged few.

The second benefit came from my thirst for reading as widely as I could. Serendipity was on my side when standing among the open library shelves, to dive into whichever book attracted my attention. Slowly, a pattern of my latent interests emerged: cognition, language, evolutionary biology, anthropology, and information theory. The common thread was a focus on structures, their functions and the dynamics underlying them. There was Piaget on genetic epistemology, Gregory Bateson and Richard Lewontin; Whorf on language, but also a bit of Leibniz; Louis Dumont with *Homo Hierarchicus*; as well as the theoretical physicist David Bohm with his ideas about an implicate order; Thomas Henry Huxley on the ethical animal and, among the classics, D'Arcy W. Thompson on growth and form. I reread Kurt Lewin's on group dynamics and delved into C. H. Waddington's three volumes on Theoretical Biology and his concept of an epigenetic landscape. This is only a selected list of authors that populated my intellectual world.

I also wanted to keep up with the young field of computational information processing (as AI was called before the name AI got indelibly attached to it at the famous Dartmouth conference in 1956) and its application to society which I had first encountered during an intensive summer course in Jerusalem with Terry Winograd, Seymour Papert, Marvin Minsky and Amos Tversky as teachers. There were so many interesting and open questions—how did cognition, information and knowledge hang together? Which role was played by language? How far could one go in borrowing from evolutionary biology and apply it to processes of societal change without falling into the trap of a rigid sociobiology? How to explain norms and under which conditions do they change? It was as if I wanted to soak up everything that sociology did not to offer—and yet, I felt, all of this was needed to gain a better understanding of how societies evolve and change. I even wrote a never published paper on verbs and nouns and how their relative dominance in language use correlates with social structures. When I recently came across Brian Arthur comparing algorithms to verbs—do this, do that, stop, repeat—it reminded me of my period of wild reading and thinking in Cambridge and it made me smile.

The third effect turned out to be more subtle and is still with me. It is my continuing deep interest in the topic of time. It all started with my arrival in Cambridge. My then considerably younger self underwent an abrupt transition into a new phase of my life. Leaving my previous life behind, I found myself from one day to the next transported from a hectic and overloaded professional agenda, compounded with turbulences in my private life, to idyllic Cambridge with no fixed obligations. I felt free to move in a rich intellectual landscape and explore it in whichever direction I wanted. How come, I asked myself, some people have so much time and others so little? Why are some able to blissfully concentrate on doing one thing at a time, while others must juggle a multitude of tasks, constantly on the verge of exhaustion? It was obvious that these questions were all about me.

Although it was not part of my original intention, I soon settled to seriously study social time. In my wild reading and thinking days, it became the structuring axis around which everything else moved. In an encounter with Edmund Leach, a renowned anthropologist and Provost of King's College, I mentioned my ongoing quest on time. As an anthropologist, he was thoroughly familiar with the many non-Western conceptions of time, embraced by indigenous people in the most remote corners of the world. We talked about cyclical time and the transformation myths of tribes in New Guinea. I even mentioned my speculative ideas about verbs and nouns. In a generous gesture, he invited me to use his private library. I could come whenever I wanted and only had to tell his secretary before. Thus, I immersed myself into whatever related to time I could lay my hands on.

Time has stayed with me as a topic ever since. It is a strand that runs through all my work, sometimes underground, like an aquafer that suddenly spurts into the open. As I will devote a whole chapter to what I call *Eigenzeit,* let me continue my non-linear path.

Leading a Double Life

The return to Vienna was a crude awakening. I felt expelled from an intellectual paradise. The prospect of remaining in Cambridge was tempting as well as realistic. It was the time when colleges were in the process of opening for women and with a Ph.D. in sociology from one of the major US universities my chances were quite good. But then came the moment when I was made to feel, for the first time in my life, the soul-crushing disadvantage of being a woman. I have often been asked how it was to be a woman in academia at a time when we were a minority and often discriminated. However, I never felt much discrimination, probably because I always succeeded to assert myself in such situations. Thanks to my mother, who taught me that I can do anything I wanted, I enjoy competition if it is fair. Intuitively,

I understood the rules of competitive games played by the boys and could easily fit in. True, the rules were not made by me, but by playing well I could beat my competitors. This time, however, was different. I was not competing with a boy nor with my ex-husband, but with the law.

After my divorce, custody of our daughter remained with me, but when I told my former husband that I would like to relocate to Cambridge with her, he refused. I understood his arguments; perhaps he understood mine, but we could not agree. This was it, as the law foresaw that a minor could only live outside Austria with consent of the father. I was forced to decide between a career in Cambridge without my daughter or returning to Vienna. What seemed to be a choice was none, and so I came back.

Universities in Austria, despite the legal and structural changes that had occurred in the wake of 1968, were still in the hands of a very conservative academic establishment. They were practically closed for outsiders like me. Luckily, I received an offer for a well-paid position to build up and direct a newly created UN-affiliated institution devoted to social welfare and social science research. I accepted and thus began my double life. One life was to direct an international institution. It meant to establish and maintain contact with policymaking and policymakers in the UN circle and to conduct internationally coordinated research projects in line with the specified objectives. The other life was devoted to my academic research with practically no other support nor an overlap with the aims of the institution I directed. As I did not want to do this secretly, I declared it to my International Board. They did not care as long as I would deliver what was expected from me.

My rich and wide-ranging intellectual experience in Cambridge had convinced me that the disciplinary boundaries of sociology were too narrow for me. I needed an interdisciplinary space, crossing disciplines and the freedom to explore whatever science had to offer. This is what science and technology studies, STS, were all about. STS had emerged from Merton's sociology of science which dealt with the institution of science and its functioning, the role of reputation, priority claims, the Matthew effect according to which prestigious institutions and scientists gain even more prestige the more they already have, and related questions, many of them still valid. STS ventured into a terrain that Mertonian sociology of science had never touched: the production of scientific knowledge. This move was later branded and often misunderstood, as the "social construction" of knowledge. The landmark study by Bruno Latour and Steve Woolgar, *Laboratory Life,* exemplified that by "following science" and observing what scientists do in the lab, it is possible to get access from a social science perspective into "science in the making."

My double life often felt like having a day job and a night job at the same time, but my priorities were clear. I expanded my STS network, ranging from Edinburgh to Paris, from Bielefeld to Amsterdam, with a supportive sprinkling from STS colleagues from MIT, Harvard, and Berkeley. I became a member of the editorial Board of the Yearbook in the Sociology of Science, which kept the initial title long after it had switched to STS and began teaching part-time an STS course in Bielefeld which could be reached by night train. But I realized that if I wanted to get a professorship at an Austrian university, I first had to obtain my *Habilitation.* This was a formal requirement consisting in submitting a major work and prove of one's teaching capability by having taught already at a national university. In addition —and this was the political part of the procedure—one had to get the necessary votes from a university committee whose composition was as much a political game as one can imagine.

The game began with finding a full professor willing to support my *Habilitation*. I did not get very far as the process was designed for insiders only. Every professor I approached assured me of his high esteem, but I had to understand that he had to give priority to the assistants who had been working for him since years. So, I decided to submit my work to the University of Bielefeld, a newly established "reform university" where a committee consisting of Peter Weingart, Niklas Luhmann, Otthein Rammstedt and Everett Mendelsohn from Harvard approved and conferred the *venia legendi* to me. Now I had the entry ticket to apply for a professorship. The only drawback was that in Austria a *Habilitation* from a foreign university was not recognized. While a lengthy procedure existed for the recognition of doctorates from abroad under the apt Latin name of "*nostrification*," nothing comparable existed for my case.

Here I was, presumably the only person in Austria with a doctorate in jurisprudence from the University of Vienna, a Ph.D. from Columbia University, and a *Habilitation* from the University of Bielefeld, but unable to obtain a *Habilitation* from an Austrian University. An unexpected invitation from Berlin came to my rescue. The recently founded Wissenschaftskolleg zu Berlin, WIKO, was in the process of appointing the first cohort of Fellows for 1981–1982. It was the first Institute for Advanced Study in Europe, modelled after the Princeton IAS. Much later, I found out that initially the WIKO Board had invited Norbert Elias, an eminent sociologist who had to flee Nazi Germany. His groundbreaking work, especially *The Civilizing Process,* received late recognition when his reputation and popularity grew throughout Europe. Due to his age, Elias did not feel like relocating to Berlin and proposed my name in his stead. I was overjoyed and took a one year leave of absence from my UN-affiliated institute. I submitted the same material that formed the basis for my Bielefeld *Habilitation* to the

University of Vienna, including the assessments from the committee that had approved it and still remember the laughable act of having to buy stamps, a kind of tax, for my application. This requirement pertained only to those who were not already employed at the university, and the tax was relatively high. In those days, one had to buy these stamps in tobacconist stores and given the high value, I had to make the round to several tobacconists until I had gathered the required amount. I glued the stamps on the envelope addressed to the University of Vienna, deposited it in the mailbox, and left for Berlin.

The committee in Vienna did not dare to overrule the approval from Bielefeld. They may never have heard of Everett Mendelsohn, but they surely knew Niklas Luhmann, a towering figure in German-speaking sociology and beyond. After a few months I was informed that I had been "habilitated." This did not include a professorship. It was merely the precondition to apply for a vacant position. Once more, I had to engage in institution building. From outside the university, I succeeded in setting up a new Institute for Science and Technology Studies and Philosophy of Science at the University of Vienna. Although the recruitment committee also played ludicrous little political games, I was appointed as the first professor of STS and director of the Institute.

Collegium Budapest (Now Defunct) and Censorship (Ongoing)

My stay as a professor at the University of Vienna, despite the long detour to get there, did not last very long. I enjoyed teaching, but as the field of STS was completely new in Austria, there was no officially approved curriculum yet. The way to attract Ph.D. students was a bit random. They came from a variety of disciplinary backgrounds and the most unusual combinations of STS with other disciplines occurred.

This widened everybody's intellectual horizon but posed additional challenges about accreditation and other bureaucratic hurdles. In short, it would take some time for STS to become fully integrated into curricula and study plans. The process to establish it not only intellectually, but also anchor it in the bureaucratic-administrative structures of the University was left to my successor and former collaborator, Ulrike Felt, who succeeded with her inexhaustible energy. Other than teaching, I decided to focus on my research and my engagement with European research policy, attend conferences and accept lecture invitations in various parts of Europe.[2]

Due to my long-standing affiliation with WIKO in Berlin, I was invited to join the efforts led by Wolf Lepenies, the Rector, and Joachim Nettelbeck, the Secretary, to set up the Collegium Budapest, Institute for Advanced Study, the first of its kind in Eastern Europe after the fall of communism. It was financed by several European governments, a Swiss foundation, and the Dutch lottery. Lengthy negotiations with the Hungarian Academy of Science and the new government followed about the building in which it would be housed. The Austrian Ministry of Science and Research agreed to grant me leave of absence from the University of Vienna for one semester every year, intended as an "in kind" contribution. For me this meant spending sufficient time in Budapest to witness from nearby how the transition to a democratic society was interpreted, exploited, and experienced differently by

2 Early on I realized that I had to choose between putting my attention and energy mainly on scientific developments in the United States or in Europe. This involved much more than following the academic literature, which of course I did. It meant attending regularly major conferences and building collaborative networks. I opted for Europe, without regrets.

various groups and how dissident intellectuals but also members of the previously powerful Academy of Science coped with the changes of the transition.

My colleagues as Permanent Fellow were János Kornai, an eminent economist whose work on the economy of scarcity had gained wide international recognition and praise. The "irregular memoirs of an intellectual journey" he wrote later are a moving account of the turbulent times he lived through and how he coped (Kornai 2006). The other was Eörs Szathmáry, a theoretical evolutionary biologist who, together with John Maynard Smith, published two landmark books on the common principles underlying the major steps in evolution. From them and through interaction with other academics I learned a lot about the previous life under communism, the aspirations harbored for the future, both in the academic world and in wider society, and the obstacles and difficulties that accompanied the economic transition process.

Collegium Budapest moved into the beautiful baroque building previously occupied by one of the institutes of the Academy of Science. Located on top of the hill of Buda with Saint Matthew's church just across the square, it offered a fantastic view of the city. The rooms provided generous space for the fellows; the Collegium had invited them to spend one academic year at the IAS, but the former library now stood empty except for two antique baroque stoves. The questions arose how to fill it. Spontaneously, I suggested that we buy eight desks and select junior fellows coming from Eastern Europe to work there. We would offer them a modest stipend but, to avoid overburdening the administration of the Collegium, leave it to them to find accommodation.

My proposal was accepted, and we began with the recruitment of junior fellows in Eastern Europe. The applications fell into two distinct categories. One part was written in perfect American English, including the style of presentation and use of the latest terminology or fashionable concepts. The others were applications written in Slavic English with the definite article often omitted and rather clumsy in style. I was able to convince my Permanent Fellow colleagues that despite these shortcomings we ought to focus on them only and disregard the first bunch. They had obviously been composed with the help of an American expat, paid by the applicant. There was no way to find out whether the ideas for the project came from the candidate or to what extent they had been influenced by a ghostwriter. This episode reminds me of today's ongoing discussion about using ChatGPT to write students' essays, or applications submitted by job seekers. Inadvertently, the candidates for a junior fellowship who had thought to be very clever by hiring a helping hand, were ahead of their time, but this is not the way how academia can or should proceed. In the end, we resorted to interview the short-listed candidates. Now, with ChatGPT looming behind every written text, we may need to do the same in the future on many more occasions, even if interviews are more time-consuming and costly.

The second category of applicants confirmed the importance of problem choice. It was surprisingly easy to detect whether the proposed research project contained an original and potentially interesting idea, however poorly it was expressed in language, structure, or style of presentation. Problems are not given, since nature does not whisper into the ear of a scientist which problem to choose, and in the social sciences every "real world" problem needs to be carefully translated into a scientific problem which can be tackled with the adequate methods and theoretical understanding. Problem choices, if they are to have an impact, must become institutionalized, contextualized, embedded, and nurtured in a collective problem space which is reconfigured from time to time (Nowotny and Leroy 2009). Obviously, the period of transition that the countries under former communistic rule underwent, brought with also a reconfiguration of the collective problem space as well as new assessment procedures for scientific publication.

The inclusion of junior fellows turned out to introduce the fresh intellectual sparks in the community of fellows that attended the conferences, weekly presentations, seminars, and public lectures we organized. The younger generation was eager to become part of the international scientific community and I encouraged them to challenge, whenever appropriate, the views, theories, methods, and findings of their more established elders, assuming a mentoring role whenever I could. It was probably in this context that I first came up with the concept of "competent rebels." To challenge what passes for conventional wisdom or established dogma, the younger generation has first to acquire the necessary competence which provides the firm anchoring space for launching their challenge. The desire to change the world or to righten the wrongs of the past, however understandable these motivations are, cannot replace it. We need not only individuals that are competent rebels, but also institutions to act as competent rebels. This is much more difficult to achieve.

All lectures at Collegium Budapest were open to the public, well attended and usually provided sufficient interesting and attractive topics for lively discussions. One such lecture was organized by a junior fellow whose research was about censorship during communism. The research project was well advanced, and she intended to present her main findings. Invitations were sent out on a routine basis, but the Rector became a bit nervous. It was to be expected that among the attendees would be some persons who had served as censors themselves. These were usually very knowledgeable academics who had interacted in a face-to-face manner with the researchers, whose work they had to scrutinize and decide what was allowed to be published or not. The event arrived and the tension in the lecture room was palpable. After all, this was a relatively small academic community and people knew each other. They also knew who their previous censor had been and, if present, could spot them. The presentation went well, and the discussion remained at a restrained academic level. No personal accusations were hurled across the room, no scandal erupted. Instead, I sensed a kind of inward-looking, collectively shared feeling of sadness, mixed with guilt that prevailed.

I may be wrong in my interpretation, but it seemed as though most participants left that evening with the shadow of the past following them. They may have asked themselves: What has been my role in this game in which almost all of us colluded? Could I have acted differently, and if so, to what avail? Could it happen again or what will happen to me now as I am faced with the ruthless liberal market in publishing my scientific work, a situation which I abhor? From now on, it obliges me to publish relentlessly, regardless of whether I think my work is mature enough for publication and to undergo evaluation exercises by people who understand little about my work and for whom only numbers, metrics and key performance indicators count.

Such soul-searching questions might even have been infiltrated by a slight whiff of nostalgia for the old system, including the censor with whom one could at least discuss one's work. Later, I asked the junior fellow how she had experienced the evening. More than anything else, she felt great relief, but she agreed that the end of the old regime was experienced as very painful, especially by those researchers who, for a variety of reasons, experienced difficulties in accepting the new rules of the game. Within the Academy of Science, I could see both factions to continue to co-exist in an uneasy relationship for quite some time.

This episode raises the question of censorship, of academic freedom and the reasons behind attributing so much power to words that strenuous efforts are undertaken to control and suppress some of them. Censorship has been practiced in the course of history until this day by authoritarian regimes and those in a position of imposing their power on others. Every authoritarian regime wants to keep control over ideas and their circulation that question their legitimacy or openly call for rebellion. They cannot tolerate dissent and soon every form of criticism is seen as treason. The Catholic Church practiced censorship to watch over the adherence to the dogmas of faith, banning as dangerous the printing and reading of ideas declared to be heretical. Like the censors in Budapest, authors had the possibility to defend their work with the ecclesiastic authorities, which effectively encouraged a self-imposed pre-censorship. The *Index Librorum Prohibitorum* (Index of Forbidden Books) lists some of the major figures of the European Enlightenment and notable scientific works, like those of Copernicus and Galileo. It was officially abolished only in 1966, although it claimed to retain its moral force.

Lately, we have seen a kind of perverse "democratization" of censorship raging in liberal democracies. With so-called "identity politics" running amok, often quite arbitrary markers of belonging or exclusion, of "us" as essentially different from "them," have been identified and reified. Claiming to speak in the name of a collective "us" against multiple other "not-us," mustering moral force with history exclusively on their side, these groups contribute to the ongoing trends of polarization, reinforced by the social media. Public discussion already eroded by retreating into the social bubbles of like-minded, makes collective life that depends on the ability to forge compromises and to conceive of a larger collectivity above narrow tribal interests, almost impossible.

In a climate of "woke" that follows "political correctness," words have ceased to function in enabling a rational and civilized discourse. When "universalism" heralded by the European Enlightenment is declared to be nothing more than a sham, even if it is admitted that principles were not followed by actual practice, a void appears in which sharing the meaning of words becomes taboo (Neiman 2023). They become weapons to wage war against opponents who are smeared by labels attached to them. Words are then stripped by the meanings they once contained and cease to be open to the multiple interpretations that need to be negotiated. Censorship is then no longer imposed by an authority from above but exercised by everyone in the battlefield. Worse, fear and paranoia take over when people no longer dare to speak what they think and the space for sharing the aspiration for common ideals like universal justice shrinks further.

Paradoxically, under an official regime of censorship, scholars and researchers can take pride in the fact that their ideas and words are deemed to have the force to threaten those in power, even if the personal price may be high. When censorship becomes everyone's right to "cancel" what is deemed to go against one's moral conviction and certain words can no longer be uttered in public, people are effectively silenced as they try to protect themselves against verbal abuse or even violence. Words lose their relevance. They become an empty shell, filled with hatred and bile with communication stripped by what enables it to function, the emergence of a *common* ground. When every form of criticism is stifled, the basis of living together is quickly eroding.

At the beginning of modern science in 17th-century Europe, official censorship imposed by the monarch as absolutist ruler applied also to the small assemblies of "natural philosophers." They gathered in academies of science to perform their experiments and openly discuss them with the intention to expose them to mutual criticism. The experiments were conducted in public for "gentlemen witnesses" to confirm the validity of an experiment. This excluded women. They did not fit into the category of being a reliable and credible witness as they were economically dependent on their husbands or fathers. Academies of science had first sprung up in Italy and soon spread to all major European capitals. They were eager to share and exchange with each other their scientific findings, ideas, and methods. However, also their correspondence fell under the regimes of censorship. Famously, the Royal Society in London succeeded to obtain a royal exemption under the provision that their correspondence abstains from "rhetoric, religion, and politics."

This voluntarily agreed self-restraint has served the natural sciences well ever since, but the social sciences and humanities continue to grapple with it, as the study of "rhetoric, religion and politics" forms an integral part of their remit. Academic freedom became enshrined in many constitutions when European countries shifted from being absolute monarchies to granting more democratic rights to their population or becoming a republic. It is intended as a shield-free scientific inquiry, including the publication of its findings, from any interference from the State. It continues to be embattled, as the number of conferences and official declarations on its behalf and support demonstrates, at international, regional, and national levels. Meanwhile, it is not only interference from the State, but also from other economic and political interests that finds itself in the eye of the storm, as recent examples show. Seemingly, it is difficult for our political leaders, but also for vested economic and other interests, to accept the fact that criticism and open discussion are the lifeblood of science, embedded in commonly accepted rules of rational discourse and empirically validated evidence. At a time when humanity faces unprecedented challenges, it is ever more urgent to redesign and reaffirm the space which science needs to thrive. This includes the criticism and its wise use.

ETH Zurich, the Collegium Helveticum, and The Branco Weiss Fellowship Program

One of the many lecture invitations I received when dividing my time between Vienna and Budapest came from ETH Zurich (Eidgenössische Technische Hochschule Zürich). I remember that I was slightly surprised to see that a larger audience than usual had come to listen. I had also been asked to meet next morning with a small committee to share my knowledge about STS as an academic field. The committee was interested to learn who the leading figures were and who was doing which kind of research. I gave them a short introduction to STS, including its potential for an international top research university like ETH Zurich. The meeting was attended also by the President of ETH, as the committee had run into difficulties recently in appointing a professor for the chair of Philosophy of Science. It had become vacant after the obligatory retirement of Paul Feyerabend, the legendary representative of "anything goes," whose 100th birthday is celebrated in 2024 (Feyerabend 1975). The big surprise came the day after my return to Vienna, when I received a phone call from the president, asking whether I would be interested to apply for the vacant position myself. As I later found out, such a procedure was not unusual, as the recruitment process at ETH is kept open until the end, enabling the president and the recruitment committee to actively search for candidates who would not otherwise apply.

These was wonderful news, but there was a problem. I could not possibly leave my position in Vienna before reaching the age of early retirement, lest I lose my pension. At best, I could try to negotiate a partial leave of absence again, but ETH surely wanted to fill the entire professorship, not only a part. So, the idea was born to find the other half, as it were. This is how Yehuda Elkana, an internationally-renowned philosopher of science and Director of The Van Leer Jerusalem Institute, and I became the "twins" of the ETH professorship for Philosophy of Science and Science Technology Studies.[3] Yehuda and I had known each other from international conferences and from my recurrent visits to the WIKO in Berlin, where he was a Permanent Fellow. He was immensely knowledgeable and the most generous person, intellectually and in human warmth, I know. We complemented each other in many ways but what we shared most was a spirit of fierce independence. The organizational arrangements were simple: Yehuda would be in Zurich during the winter semester, leaving the more pleasant months of the year to me. We agreed to be present for several days at each other's term at least twice to coordinate our teaching and related activities, but mainly because we enjoyed discussing, working, and keeping an open house together. We shared an apartment and with Yehuda being an excellent cook, this somewhat unusual arrangement became an attractive and recognized feature of the scientific and intellectual life in Zurich.

Thus, Yehuda and I were also drawn also into setting up the Collegium Helveticum, the Swiss version of an Institute for Advanced Study. The idea originated from Adolf Muschg, a well-known writer and professor of literature at ETH Zurich. The *Sternwarte,* an architectural jewel built be Gottfried Semper as the first observatory of ETH, stood empty and soon became an intellectually lively forum for the natural sciences, social sciences, and humanities to meet. Yehuda and I created a small graduate college for Ph.D. students from ETH and the University of Zurich. They would spend one year working on their dissertation, surrounded (and creatively distracted)

---

3 I still have one of our business cards, with Yehuda's name, email, and phone on one side, and mine on the other.

by world renowned guests from the academic, literary, and artistic world. Twice a week everyone was participating in seminars and discussions, presenting their work, and learning from each other. The *Kollegiat:innen* (fellows) would also cook on these days and the meals became one of the many highlights of what an intellectual communal life could be like. The importance of the location and architectural space that enables or stifles such interactions is generally neglected. But here we were, in Semper's Observatory, occupying the beautifully restored rooms in which Professor Wolff, the first professor of astronomy of ETH and the discoverer of the sunspots, had worked and lived, assisted as a bachelor by his sister. During springtime, we enjoyed the garden of old roses on the ground where some 140 years ago the observational instruments had been rolled out.

We organized a series of international conferences and lectures open to the academic world and to the public, carefully selecting topics which were at the forefront of scientific developments or at the interface between disciplines. Without ever mentioning it, I made sure that each of the conference panels included at least one woman. One year after it was founded I took over as Director of the Collegium Helveticum and look back with joy on the atmosphere filled with a vibrant and enriching transdisciplinarity, the opening of the sciences towards the arts and literature, and the unique communal academic life it gave rise to. As Yehuda had to retire before me due to the age limit, I stepped in to fill the other half of the professorship. The years at ETH Zurich gave me the opportunity to create an inter- and transdisciplinary space which I could fill in ways I thought best. Among others, I launched a group for transdisciplinary studies which resonated especially with the recently established Department for Environmental Studies and nascent attempts in Switzerland to better connect science and civil society.

One of the many rewarding encounters at ETH Zurich was with Branco Weiss, a successful tech entrepreneur and philanthropist who had come to Switzerland as a child with his mother fleeing from the Nazis. Branco had a wide range of interests, especially in people. He attended many events of the Collegium Helveticum, and even some of my lectures. When the date of my retirement from ETH approached, he suggested that we should find a way for me to stay and continue my work with young scientists, as I had done at the Collegium. This is how we came up with the idea of the "Society-in-Science" Branco Weiss Fellowship Program. It offered a fellowship for young researchers in the life sciences to pursue "society" in their "science." The idea was to find exceptional individuals with a personal vision of a scientific project who were keen to go beyond mainstream. The terms of the fellowship were as unconventional as was the profile of those it was seeking to attract. Neither the location nor the amount of funding was specified in advance. Fellows were free for up to five years to follow their unconventional ideas and to render "society" alive into their "science."

Recruiting young scientists for the fellowship program brought with it many insights into the tight structuring of academic careers, the pressure young scientists felt and the difficulties they faced if they wanted to open their research to broader societal dimensions. We were looking for young scientists daring to go beyond mainstream, and we found some exceptional and impressive young researchers whose career and scientific outlook we supported. With one of them, Giuseppe Testa, I later published *Naked Genes. Reinventing the Human in the Molecular Age.* In the book we examine the interaction of the latest advances in the life sciences with the social and political reconfigurations in contemporary societies (Nowotny and Testa 2011). For me, working on the book was the kind of rewarding, but rare, collaboration between a natural and social scientist which allows to combine scientific accuracy with insightful, yet sharp societal interpretation. Since then, Giuseppe has advanced in his impressive scientific career and now leads the Neurogenomics research program at the Human Technopole in Milano, studying the molecular mechanisms underlying intellectual disabilities and autism. My involvement with The Branco Weiss Fellowship program ended when I left Zurich, as the demands grew to spend more time on policy engagements at EU level. The fellowship program was bequeathed by Branco in 2010 with a sizeable donation to ETH Zurich, where it continues to attract postdocs with unconventional projects outside the scientific mainstream.

Looking back at my academic trajectory, it is perhaps more understandable why I consider contingencies so important. Repeatedly, I found myself in situations where, in retrospect, it is clear that "It is so. It could be otherwise" (Nowotny 2000). Partly, my non-linear trajectory is connected to the fact that I followed my husband to New York and returned with him to Europe, which entailed switching career directions. This happens more often to women than to men, but it was my choice and enriched my life. I feel immensely privileged when comparing myself to some of my former colleagues who had chosen the smooth, linear career path. Many ended up in increasingly more narrow specialization, which breeds the frustration emanating from more of the same. Partly, however, my non-linear trajectory is also the outcome of continuously navigating around the mainstream, being an insider and an outsider, sometimes simultaneously.

I was—and still am—engaged in institution building, not because this was my ambition, but because it was a necessity. I needed an institutional base and an infrastructure to pursue my research questions. It helps to know about the functioning mechanisms behind policymaking and the circumstances in which policymakers act. It is also a great asset to have a sense of timing, to know when to act, to delay or to renounce. Perhaps my familiarity with changing weather conditions in the Alps taught me to be very attentive to the necessity of having to change plans. I always considered the ability to take a decision a huge privilege to be treasured.

Throughout my non-linear trajectory I continued to learn about institutions; "how they think" (Douglas 1986) and function; how to set them up, run them, fund them—and leave them once I am no longer needed as the founder or a founding member. I know that the moment has come, at least for me, when the "routinization of charisma" sets in and the excitement about the visions and ambitions it incorporates settle down. Ideally, the phase of consolidation begins then. This is also hard work, but I prefer the pioneering phase, in line with my mantra about embracing uncertainty: not to be afraid of the yet unknown, but to draw strength and inspiration from entering new territory; to trust the hidden forces of chance and the cunning of uncertainty; whether it manifests itself in the form of serendipity, or in situations where it is too difficult to make a seemingly rational choice based on evidence that can only come from the past. It is about keeping the future open, the reward we get for accepting that the future is inherently uncertain, for it can always be otherwise.

II.

Moving between Science and Policymaking

During my annual stays as Visiting Professor at Nanyang Technical University (NTU) in Singapore (more about this later), my friend Balázs Gulyás introduced me over one of several unforgettable dinners to Sydney Brenner, Nobel Laureate in physiology or medicine. On one occasion, Sydney Brenner shared one of his succinct insights: "Mathematics deals with the perfect, physics deals with the optimal and biology with the satisfactory." I could not hold myself and replied: "Sydney, you forgot the social sciences, or do you consider them not to be sciences?" Without waiting for an answer, I continued, "and the social sciences deal with the messy" (Nowotny 2017). If this is so, dealing with science policy and research policy is at least as messy. Every country, every funding institution, every university department does it in a different way, but all are involved. Science policymaking is as diverse as any other policy, but not as universal as science claims to be.

I was early drawn into science policy through a major controversy. Although it erupted in Austria, it shared many features with similar controversies worldwide, revealing the ongoing tensions between "society" and "science" in different constellations. Controversies have their own dynamics. They erupt at unpredictable moments, involving previously unconcerned citizens and scientists are drawn into it and suddenly become concerned. Although "science" is implicated, politics is never far away. Like other political struggles, the ways in which a socio-scientific or socio-technical controversy unfolds is shaped by the reaction it elicits from the wider environment. This can be the government or political parties that align or oppose; opportunistic media that take sides or excessive actions by the police that may lead to increase the number of opponents. Scientists, although they have internalized to draw a demarcation line between their science and politics, can no longer abstain when they are obliged to take a stand and defend what they do. Citizens mobilize when they feel their way of life, or their vision of the kind of society they want to live in, are challenged. Under such circumstances, science becomes a visible target, although the roots of the underlying conflict usually lie elsewhere.

In the early 1970s, nuclear power plants were under construction in several European countries. Bruno Kreisky, chancellor of Austria at the time, received a concerned phone call from his friends in Sweden, warning him that nuclear energy might become the target of a nascent environmental movement that could oppose further construction. The newly established Ministry of Science and Research had an unusually high number of civil servants coming from the natural sciences and one of the director generals, a physicist, who was tasked to look after the matter, decided to launch an information campaign on nuclear energy. The plan was to discuss the scientific arguments pro and contra nuclear energy first among scientists, who were to be selected in equal number being pro and contra, and later with the public at large. As one can see, this approach was impeccably scientific, carried by the conviction that all it takes is to convince the public of reasonable, scientific arguments. A friend of mine was one of the young physicists working in the ministry and told me about the plan. I proposed to conduct an empirical study of a "controversy in the making," which would give me full access to a live experiment while the government might find it useful to get an independent analysis and documentation of the entire consultation process.

My proposal was accepted and allowed me to gain firsthand insights into how scientists dealt with the controversy, how policymaking was taking shape and how the public that insisted on being heard would react. Not surprisingly, the information campaign did not quite go according to plan. I gained valuable insights into the dynamics of such a controversy, the tensions involved and their underlying causes and how the concepts of risk changed in the process. For the government, however, the experiment ended with an unexpected outcome, as the opening of the almost finished nuclear plant was defeated in a referendum (Nowotny 1979). It kindled my long-lasting interest in following the genesis and unfolding of scientific-technical controversies in society—from nuclear energy to GMOs; from genetic testing to the rapidly multiplying environmental concerns, on to the recent COVID pandemic and anti-vax movements. I followed by tracing the actors and their networks; the different concepts of risks they deployed and how these concepts changed; the importance of trust and how quickly it could vanish; the tensions, misunderstandings and the hapless communication undertaken by "science" once "society" felt empowered to "talk back to science." These controversies and the tensions underpinning them displayed different features of policymaking than those that would play out normally, but they too belong to policymaking.

One of several international organizations hosted in Austria is the International Institute for Applied Systems Analysis (IIASA). Through my study of the nuclear power controversy, I got in touch with a group at IIASA working on risk, which led to the publication of a report I wrote for the IIASA series. Although I never was formally associated with IIASA, I became part of a group of colleagues working on energy and environmental issues, who have become friends until this day. I attended conferences and got to know most of IIASA's directors. IIASA's work was geared towards the applied side of what were already then defined to be the global challenges. Issues of policy advice, the use of evidence, and how to engage with policymakers were part of our ongoing conversations and were fed by the experience of participating in many of the ongoing international conferences in this field.

Meanwhile, another policy arena was taking shape at European level. Most, but not all, were under the umbrella of the European Commission expanding its political remit and areas of competence. In the beginning, the now defunct European Science Foundation (ESF), composed of representatives of the national research funding organizations, played an important role for launching and coordinating research projects at the European level. During a visit in Paris, an ESF search committee approached me and asked whether I would be willing to chair the ESF Social Science Committee, which I gladly accepted. I was not aware that the members of the committee were appointed by their respective national funding organizations. In contrast, I was a complete outsider and I understood only later that it was my scientific independence that had appealed to the search committee to approach me.

Whatever were the procedures through which the search committee succeeded to get me elected as chair, I arrived for the first meeting in Uppsala as an outsider unknown to most members of the Social Science Committee. Many must have felt that I had been imposed on them. I did not expect a warm welcome, but the reception was rather frosty. I was well prepared, having carefully studied all the documents. Still, I had to muster all my social skills and intellectual acumen to convince them that I could chair in a productive, decisive, and convivial way. Looking back at this episode, I realize that it was one of those situations where either one learns to swim, or one sinks. Intuitively, I listened attentively to everybody who wanted to speak, without letting anybody speak too much. At the same time, I had to extract a common thread, find possible compromise solutions, and unobtrusively guide the discussion in the direction I saw fit. During the entire meeting, I followed my sense of where we should be heading. Trusting my intuition, I summarized at the end and drew the conclusions, which were unanimously agreed upon.

What I learned during this day in Uppsala has served me well ever since. I am good at chairing a group and acting as a moderator and have had numerous occasions in different settings and in differently composed groups to practice this art. My experience chairing many EU committee meetings may have been one reason I was asked much later to become Chair of the European Research Advisory Board (EURAB), the highest body to advise the European Commission on RTI (Research, Technology and Innovation) policies. EURAB had forty-five members, half of them coming from industry and the other half from academia, with the chair as arbiter in case of a split vote. Before I took over, the two factions would convene amongst themselves prior to the meeting. I told them that I wanted nothing of this kind. Either we were able to discuss matters and succeed in bringing diverging interests together, allowing us subsequently to speak with one voice, or we were reducing ourselves to a mere discussion club. It worked.

One of our recommendations concerned the establishment of a new funding body at the EU level devoted entirely to fund basic research in a genuine bottom-up mode, Principal Investigator (PI)-

centered and based on the sole criteria of "scientific excellence." The idea of a European Research Council (ERC) to fund basic research at the EU level had been under discussion for some time. It was a radical proposal, enthusiastically supported by scientists everywhere in Europe, but difficult to achieve as it entailed a complete reversal of EU policy. Practically all EU funded projects were geared towards applied research, many of them carried out by large consortia who had to carefully consider "geographical balance" in their composition. This was in accordance with the European Treaties that foresaw funding only "to strengthen the economic competitiveness of Europe." This was applied research, while funding basic science was left to member states. Although the demand to fund basic research at the EU level had been a high priority for scientists for many years, I wish I could say that the well-founded arguments by scientists to reverse this strategy won out, but they were not sufficient.

Politicians only became interested in changing policy when the wave of denationalization of industries set in, forcing previously protected companies to suddenly compete on global markets. The long-term fundamental science knowledge that industry needed to maintain its competitive edge came from the universities in member states. What would happen if national funding for basic research carried out in universities decreased? The first to notice were the small Scandinavian countries who put a reversal of the existing EU policy on the agenda. Immediately, this triggered a flurry of activities among scientists in which numerous scientific organizations participated. The political establishment was still reluctant and such a major policy shift would take time and considerable effort. Nevertheless, in 2002 a major conference took place under the rotating Danish EU presidency with the title "Towards a European Research Area: Do We Need a European Research Council?" The question mark stood for the doubt about such an institution and the official reluctance, underlining the wavering hesitancy of policymakers, while the scientific community was enthusiastic.

Setting up the European Research Council was discussed in various policy circles. Like other scientists involved in policy advice, I took part in many of these meetings. Together with Wilhelm Krull, Secretary General of the Volkswagen Foundation, we published an article in the journal *Nature* entitled "The ERC—an idea whose time has come" (Krull and Nowotny 2004). The window of opportunity was very narrow, as the preparations for the next multiannual EU Framework Programme were moving towards closure. Admittedly, EURAB's voice had some extra weight, as we could show to the European Commission that also industry backed the idea. In the EURAB inner circle we used all possible personal connections to influence politicians. One of them, Lord Sainsbury, the UK Minister responsible for science and an important political voice at the EU level, publicly stated at a crucial conference in Dublin that he had changed his mind after being persuaded by the arguments of scientists. The person who convinced him the day before was one of the EURAB members I had asked to speak to him.

Some called it "a miracle" when the European Research Council was established in 2006 with the mission to fund "frontier research" based on the principle of "scientific excellence" only. The design and strategy of the ERC was entrusted to a group of twenty-two scientists and scholars, chosen by a small committee chaired by Lord Patten from a list of 400 names. They constituted the ERC Scientific Council and saw themselves as pioneers in setting up a European funding organization for fundamental research in Europe, run "by scientists, for scientists." The ERC began its work immediately and prepared for the official opening in January 2007. I was elected Vice-President and from March 2010 until December 2013 served as ERC President. While the EU legislation left all strategic decisions to set up and run the ERC to my colleagues and me, the implementation of our decisions was given to an ERC Executive Agency working under the rules of the European Commission. Inevitably, this generates tensions as the strategic decisions can never be neatly separated from their implementation. Some of these tensions were resolved over time, while others last until this day. In the eyes of many Commission officials the ERC continues to be regarded as an "anomaly," as the decisions involving an annual budget amounting to €2.2 billion in 2023 are made by a group of independent scientists, who are not completely under the control of the Commission.

I look back on the years I spent for and with the ERC with great satisfaction on what has been achieved. The ERC has become the unrivaled success story for funding basic research in the EU. It is open to participation from outside Europe and has become the envy of scientists in many parts of the world. I hope that politicians and policymakers will understand that fundamental research indeed is an "anomaly" in the sense that the outcome of research is inherently uncertain and cannot be planned. It takes time, but the "usefulness of useless knowledge," as Abraham Flexner called it, has been vindicated numerous times (Flexner and Dijkgraaf 2017). Basic research remains the foundation of scientific knowledge, without which the pipeline leading to beneficial applications would soon dry up.

I discovered that in my dealings with the Commission services, I had an advantage over many of my colleagues from the natural sciences. When we met obstacles, usually I was able to distinguish the institutional structures from the persons who were working within them. I saw the constraints imposed by institutions and the rules that governed them, but also noticed the loopholes and workarounds without which no institution can function. When we were told that we could not proceed as we wanted, as this was against the rules, several of my colleagues took it very personally and became frustrated. It was a clash of cultures. The Commission was pervaded by a culture of control, while the scientific community espouses a culture of trust. Scientists knew that basic research needs to be shielded against the pressures of immediate and instrumental usefulness, but Commission officials often mistook this for arrogance, for wanting to be "different" or as refusal to fit into the bureaucratic mold designed to be the same for all. Undoubtedly, my background in STS helped me to contribute to the success the ERC became in the quite unique policy environment that "Bruxelles" occupies in Europe.

With hindsight, I realize how well my scholarly pursuits and field research had prepared me to bring my knowledge and skills to help to build up and lead the ERC. I felt like an anthropologist who had spent considerable time with the tribe of scientists I had got to know quite well through my research. What had been "informants" in the field before, now were my colleagues. In practice, scientists constitute many different tribes that have their own rituals, ancestors, and heroes. They have different customs and display different behavior. At the ERC Scientific Council, we encouraged all panels that we set up to evaluate the applications for funding to base the panel's decisions on following the scientific or scholarly culture of the field covered by the panel's expertise. This goes beyond knowing the state-of-the art and covers publication standards and habits, what counts as evidence or what a typical career structure looks like. But differences in behavior were to be found also between panels. For instance, the panel of economists was the only one who enjoyed voting to reach a decision. All other panels strove to reach consensus by argument and persuasion. Taking a vote was considered to be a last, almost desperate, act.

One of the unique features of the ERC is that it includes the humanities and social sciences. From the very beginning there was never any doubt or a discussion about this and when it came to the distribution of funding for the three domains of physical sciences and engineering, life sciences, and social sciences and humanities (SH), we agreed that it should follow demand. Initially, SH received 15% of the total budget, which now has risen to around 25%. This inclusive approach towards science is anchored in the European concept of science in the sense of the 19th-century term *Wissenschaft* when Germany was the world's leader. It should be recalled that all great scientists from that period had a solid humanistic education, and the humanities enjoyed a high prestige. The inclusive terminology is reflected in the Scandinavian and Dutch languages, while the plural, the *les sciences* or *le scienze,* is prevalent in Southern Europe. It was only after WW2 in the Anglo-American use of language that the term science refers exclusively to the natural sciences. Unfortunately, this was reinforced by the misguided trope of the "two cultures" that originated from a specific division in the British education system and its prolongation in public administration.

I realized only much later how much my previous empirical research into the functioning of the science system and the changes it underwent helped me to understand better what I experienced in practice. When we studied the aftermath of the discovery of high-temperature superconductivity mentioned above, we wanted to know how this unexpected moment of high promise that challenged the conventional scientific wisdom and aroused expectations of untold technological marvels, would translate into policy. We set out to investigate how researchers, policymakers, industry, the media, and through them, the public reacted to this highly publicized event. How effectively could a sudden opportunity that called for investments not foreseen in annual budgets be exploited? Which research policies and funding institutions proved flexible and adaptable, which ones were hidebound and brittle? By comparing at first hand the policy responses in Germany, Austria, Switzerland, and the Netherlands, we investigated the national diversity across culturally similar countries and the extent to which basic research is still largely supported and shaped by national governments. In the end, none of the mesmerizing promises were fulfilled. High-Temperature Superconductivity (HTS) research settled and eventually returned to "normal science."

Reviewing the book *Selling Science*, which I coauthored with Ulrike Felt, for the journal *Nature*, John Ziman wrote: "Its well-informed, dispassionate analysis of the reaction of science to the bombshell of high-temperature superconductivity arrives at a radical conclusion, which all scientists need to take very seriously indeed" (Ziman 1997). What was our radical conclusion? Our focus was on science undergoing a major transformation and adapting to changing circumstances. Technological promise was becoming the main criterion for "good science." We analyzed the pressure on basic research to react rapidly to still vague promises. Basic science had become what we called an "extended laboratory," open on every side to its political, economic, and social environment and the expectations that came from there. Individual creativity was still cherished but giving way to collective modes of working. Scientists had to spend an extraordinary amount of time outside the lab to open extra-scientific channels of communication. They engaged in what we called "scientizing"—carrying out a wide range of activities aligned with the forces that shape the research and funding landscape.

For instance, scientists claimed that national funding support would be key to the economic competitiveness of the country. Although they knew that this was widely exaggerated, they were convinced that this rhetoric was justified to obtain funding. Egged on by the media, politicians accepted these claims, and then needed reassurance that they were right to do so. This led to a credibility game where the bench researchers were exposed to harsh realities that are seldom publicly aired. Under the banner of national competitiveness and globalization, ours became a case study of "selling basic science." It showed how fragile research policy could be, subject to multiple influences and trapped by its own policy rhetoric, the "stories" told by the media, and the political decisions that were taken—all driven by claims about future achievements.

The conclusions we drew were never read by the many scientists who, following Ziman's recommendation, should take them seriously. Nor did they reach many policymakers. At best, the book occupies a respected niche in the contemporary history of science and among readers in the STS community. Science and research policy resembles politics in the sense that it can be quite ephemeral. In retrospect, it makes the success of the ERC all the more remarkable, as basic research became firmly institutionalized at the highest possible level, that of European research policy. The ERC sets the "gold standard" for evaluating excellence in science and exerts lasting influence on the research policies in national contexts. On a personal level, I can only guess that perhaps my experience in analyzing what happened *After the Breakthrough: The Emergence of High-Temperature Superconductivity as a Research Field* sharpened my dedicated efforts to make the ERC the success it became.

Mode 2 Knowledge Production

Another foray into analyzing the world of policymaking and the turbulent changes that occurred through the social transformation of knowledge production was a sustained collaborative effort at the beginnings of the 1990s. The Swedish Council for Research and Planning in Stockholm, FRN, conceived and funded a project, managed by Michael Gibbons, Director of the Science Policy Research Unit at the University of Sussex. The aim was to investigate ongoing transformative changes in the production of scientific knowledge, covering the natural sciences and technology, as well as the social sciences and humanities. Our mode of working was unusual. We met as a group at regular intervals for several days in nice and remote occasions for brainstorming and discussion. We had a fixed timetable for discussion, rewarded by excellent dinners in the evening. Once we were back home, we worked on assigned tasks between our meetings, which were circulated among the other members to comment, amend, or add from their perspective and experience. Care was taken that none of us took intellectual ownership of a particular idea or chapter. To our own surprise, it worked. The result was a collectively written book, although the final version was left to Michael to be unified (Gibbons et al. 1994).

We came up with the concept of Mode 2 knowledge production, in contrast to the traditional Mode 1 which essentially follows the rules and norms of disciplinary science, but not replacing it. Our claim was that the new mode operated within specific contexts of application in that problems are not set within a disciplinary framework. Therefore, the common definition of the problem is crucial, and time must be set aside to reach such a shared definition. Typically, working in Mode 2 is carried out in transdisciplinary forms of organization. These are essentially transient and multiform and not necessarily found in conventional university structures. Since a close interaction among heterogeneous social actors, including some from outside academia, is involved, it renders knowledge production more socially accountable and uses a wider range of criteria in judging quality control. Overall, the process of knowledge production would become more reflexive, affecting at a deeper level what counts as "good science."[1]

The concept of Mode 2 was eagerly embraced by many policymakers and by those in academic disciplines that felt it represented what they were doing. It was criticized by academic colleagues for lack of a sufficient empirical basis, despite our emphasis that we wrote an essay intended to stimulate and provoke discussion on ongoing changes. It was attacked by the academic defenders of the cognitive and social norms of traditional ways of defining science. Overall, the reception and wide diffusion of the concept of Mode 2 triggered long-lasting discussions about the "contract" between "science" and "society." It even stimulated some adventurous policymakers to launch transdisciplinary funding programs, acknowledging inspiration by Mode 2. Once the dust raised by the initial reactions and provocation had settled, I wrote a sequel as first author with Peter Scott and Michael Gibbons. *Re-Thinking Science. Knowledge and the Public in an Age of Uncertainty* clarified and refined the original ideas and developed the argument further by including recent changes in the relationship between science and society.

The concept of Mode 2 found its presumably final resting place in the Elgar Encyclopedia of Inter- and Transdisciplinarity. Together with Peter Scott we explain the popularity of using wider concepts like modes of knowledge production as reflecting the recognition of the interconnectedness of all aspects of knowledge generation. They are upheld by core beliefs of science that are expressed in terms of policy, for instance, changes in the forms of research assessment and attempts

1 A good overview and reflexive assessment of Mode 2 is to be found in Helga Nowotny, Peter Scott and Michael Gibbons, "Mode 2 Revisited: The New Production of Knowledge," *Minerva* 41 (September 2003): 179–194.

to measure the impact of research. New phenomena, such as open science, pre-prints, grey and fake literature, big data, and AI increase the indeterminacy about the status of scientific publications and, especially, the impact of artificial intelligence that pose new challenges, both to policy and theory (Nowotny and Scott 2024).

In sketching some of my excursions into the overall messiness of science policymaking, I have deliberately eschewed the better-known interactions that continue to shape the relationship between "science" and "politics." Nor have I dwelled on my witnessing the advantage that informal relationships between scientists and political decision-makers often have, compared to the institutionalized form of scientific advice. Obviously, both are needed. Instead, I have emphasized the entanglement between the different cultures of trust, values and beliefs that shape the expectations of future achievements on all sides. Science policy is the outcome of ongoing negotiations, tensions, and contradictions that keep changing in accordance with the economic, technological, and political forces that feed the dynamics of their interactions. I found that the core beliefs of science are surprisingly resilient, despite ongoing confrontations, internal contradictions, and pressure from outside.

These pressures are likely to increase as we may be entering a new phase. The impact of disinformation and fake news undermining the institutions of liberal democracies will also affect science, as we have already seen during the pandemic. It is indicative that in liberal democracies trust or mistrust in science correlates with trust or mistrust in democratic institutions. The messiness is likely to get even more messy. Maybe the time has come to recuperate and redefine the 19th-century notion of *Wissenschaft* (the systematic pursuit of knowledge, learning, and scholarship, especially as contrasted with its application), which always included the humanities and social sciences as an integral part of a comprehensive striving of exploring and understanding the natural and the social world. The split in the Anglo-American usage of the term science, which exclusively refers to the natural sciences, while the humanities and social sciences are often relegated to secondary status or not being considered sciences at all, must be overcome.

The challenges humanity faces today are huge. They go beyond our fraught and dysfunctional relationship with nature. The level of aggression within the human species must be seen in the context of the technological sophistication which the means of destruction at our disposal have attained. We are at the crossroad of outsourcing to digital entities many of our cognitive capabilities, moving towards the automation of prediction and decision-making based on algorithms. "Algorithms of anxiety" are reshaping everything, from our personal lives to the automation of warfare (Elliott 2024). We urgently need to find new ways of boosting human cooperation and to strengthen cooperative bonds at every level of society, from the personal to the institutional, and relations between societies at the global level. It is unlikely that this urgency and related challenges can be met by more interdisciplinarity alone, important as it is. At the dawn of modern science and amazed by the visible progress that was achieved, the hopes of the Enlightenment were pinned for a brief moment on *"les progrès morales,"* enabling progress in science to lead also to moral progress (in the plural). These aspirations were soon dashed and abandoned. And yet, if not by thoroughly rethinking and redefining *Wissenschaft* in an inclusive and integrative sense, how will humanity be able to find common ground for a normative order in tune with its scientific knowledge and technological prowess to guarantee a life in human dignity for the nine billion on this planet?

Digression 1

Not everything I strove to achieve went smoothly, even if the institutional preconditions seemed right. When Yehuda and I arrived at ETH Zurich we were welcomed, but when we started to put our ideas into practice and opened the Collegium Helveticum's carefully composed lecture program for the entire ETH community and beyond, we met with a mixture of complacency and occasionally passive hostility. When I tried to set up a Master program for STS at the University of Vienna, I was told that this would require a change in the law and that no exception could be made for me. Indeed, it took years to achieve, but by that time I had already left. Establishing the ERC in the first years brought with it a continuous struggle with the Commission services, many of whom considered the twenty-two scientists of the ERC Scientific Council as intruders that did not fit into the existing bureaucratic order. I was often confronted with what the legal services allegedly maintained not to be possible, but despite my efforts to discuss openly with them, such an encounter never materialized. At one point regarding an important matter, I got so upset that I told my interlocutor that I would resign, but that the day after an article would be published in the *Financial Times* explaining the reasons for my resignation. It worked, and the argument from the legal services simply vanished.

These examples show how intrinsically institutions are intertwined with people and how differently people behave in different institutional contexts. Laws can be changed, but it takes a long time, many actors must be mobilized, and their interests aligned. Rules can be changed, but again it needs patience and quite a lot of effort. People can be convinced to change their behavior and their attitudes, and this is where ways of communicating with them enter. I have learned to never trust the first impression I get from meeting someone for the first time. We all form a first impression in a process akin to Daniel Kahneman's System 1, the fast way of thinking that is near-instantaneous and happens intuitively (Kahneman 2011). Therefore, I immediately switch on my System 2 for thinking slowly and tell it to be as open as possible for receiving additional information from the person I just met. I am very much aware that what I can grasp about the other person is only a tiny slice, a superficial glance of somebody who has decided to present him- or herself to me in a specific way. During further interaction, I will gain additional information which is always conditioned by the way how I act and react in the social interchange that follows. It feels like a dance. There are better and worse dancing partners and sometimes one cannot choose. But it remains a dance.

This has served me well in establishing a level playing field, marked by openness, fairness, and respect. Gradually, I obtain more information about the other person, and when I am communicating with a group, also about the relationships that exist between them. This has enabled me to practice what are called diplomatic skills, a friendly way of dealing with people, putting them at ease and inviting them to contribute towards the aims of the interaction. In contrast to a diplomat, however, I am my own free agent. I know the direction and what I want to achieve. I remain focused on my aim and do not let go. But I can do this only because of my strong sense of independence, both in the scientific and personal sense. Most likely, it goes back to my innate skepticism towards every form of authority. My sense of realism guides me in accepting it, at least towards the outside, whenever it is necessary to keep me out of harms way. But cognitively and emotionally I feel immune against accepting authority and authoritative claims only because they come from those in a position of authority. Rules can be followed, but also subverted, one only has to know when. Skepticism is an epistemic virtue. Science, and studying science and what scientists do, are a good place to cultivate it and this is one of the reasons why I like to do what I do.

III.

Women—and Men—in Science

On the occasion of the 40th anniversary of the Wissenschaftskolleg zu Berlin, Rector Barbara Stollberg-Rilinger invited me to give the annual welcome address for the new fellows.[1] It was unavoidable that I would also speak about how it felt to be a woman among the many *Germanisten* (German Studies scholars) who were the fellows during the first year. There were only two women and my colleague, a literary scholar from Israel, announced that she was pregnant. I was deeply shocked to hear these scholars discuss whether a pregnant woman can be a fellow and spontaneously decided to change the topic of my lecture. It turned out to be a remarkable event. The lecture had the title "How Male is Science?" and was open to the public. Most men in

---

1 Helga Nowotny und Barbara Stollberg-Rilinger, "Berliner Empfang 2021 mit" (speech, Berlin, September 27, 2021), Wissenschaftskolleg zu Berlin, https://www.wiko-berlin.de/wikothek/multimedia/berliner-empfang-2020-mithelga-nowotny-und-barbara-stollberg-rilinger.

the audience kept quiet, either because they were clever or indifferent. Those who spoke ran into a fierce opposition from the feminists who were present. My WIKO co-fellows, however, thought that the topic was neither scientific nor of any concern to them.

Later, Karin Hausen, an eminent social historian, approached me to organize a conference on the topic, which was turned into a book with the same title, *Wie männlich ist die Wissenschaft?* (Hausen and Nowotny 1986). For the conference we had invited women from different scientific disciplines to speak about their experience, but also four or five men whom we asked to comment the papers given by women. They all were sympathetic to feminism. However, during the week two of them approached me separately and told me that only now they realized what it meant to be in a minority as a man in a women's conference, and how women must constantly feel when they are in a conference dominated by men. Intellectually, they could analyze it, but emotionally they felt unable to cope, and told me that they would leave. Maybe this is a reminder how much of a society's cultural norms, socialization, and feelings are involved when doing science. In view of the many great and wonderful things science enables us to do and understand, it is easy to forget that it is—above all—also a social endeavor.[2]

Much has changed since, and much for the better. Women occupy top academic positions, and their numbers are rising even among Nobel Laureates, admittedly from a historically low base. Women among the ERC Starting and Consolidator grantees have risen to

---

2 The role played by the successive waves of feminism in achieving improvements for women in science still awaits closer analysis. For a first-hand testimony by one of the pioneers, see the memoir by Evelyn Fox Keller, *Making Sense of My Life in Science*. Amherst: Modern Memoirs, 2023.

almost 40% in 2021 while the comparatively modest 25% among the ERC Advanced grantees in reality represent the biggest jump ever from 10% in 2014, reflecting the growing percentage of women full professors in Europe. Yet, these figures do not answer the question of what keeps women from reaching equality in science and to change the still existing power imbalance in academia. Many of the obstacles are well known. So are the measures and policies to attain a situation where biases are held in check and discrimination no longer occurs. Open discrimination has decreased significantly, but unconscious bias and other hurdles persist. The "leaky pipeline" continues to leak, which is an alarming signal that the social system of science as a system is not only letting women down but fails to live up to its own standards.

It is well known that women scientists, holding other factors constant, publish less. The most plausible reason is that many women are hesitant to publish unless they are convinced that they have something to say, while men have no reservation to publish as much as possible in as many small slices they can. This is favored by a reward system tilted towards quantitative indicators and other measurable proxies for quality in scientific productivity. Recent initiatives in Europe, like the Agreement on Reforming Research Assessment coalition, signed already by fifty-one funding organizations and universities, were triggered not by the aim to attract and retain more women in science, but by the growing awareness of the dysfunctionalities of the peer review system that have become too serious to ignore. Nevertheless, they are a step in the right direction and women are likely to benefit.

Many of the concerns regarding research and higher education address problems that are not specific to women only. The pressure resulting from the accelerated production of scientific output and the excessive accountability procedures do not only impact women. The temporal reordering of universities with a tightening of deadlines and schedules and the numerous prescriptions performed through various temporal regimes cause academics to experience considerable tensions and unease. By looking carefully at the temporal fabric of academic lives, an interwoven picture of the multiple temporal orders emerges and how they impact women and men at the different stages of their career.

Ulrike Felt, my former collaborator and successor at the University of Vienna, proposed the sensitizing concept of "epistemic living spaces," in which the contradictory demands, temporal inconsistencies and tensions of reconciling life, academic careers, and epistemic achievements are brought together (Felt 2009). They differ in accordance with career stage, fields, institutional cultures, work environment and supportive networks. Based on many interviews with researchers and attentive to the narratives through which meanings and values of academic knowledge/work and its relation to society are articulated, circulated, and exchanged, she has captured the environment that researchers inhabit and that they consider relevant for the knowledge they wish to generate and the lives they wish to live. This is no longer about women's lives in academia, comparing them to their male colleagues. Rather it is about academic lives and the epistemic living spaces they inhabit, the entangled mixture of knowing and living—together.

Wherever one looks, there is no way to deny that science is a social system and thus an integral part of the society that cultivates and supports it. Whatever disadvantages women suffer in a society, they will spill over into disfavoring them also in science. The scientific norm of universalism and impartiality notwithstanding, biases and stereotypes that exist in society will creep into every evaluation procedure and assessment regime. They have been designed to favor those the system wants to admit and work against those it will exclude. The dream of the feminists of the 1970s, that a gender-blind and color-blind science is possible, may have been naïve, but it persists as an ideal that continues to encounter a harsh reality in practice. The selective filters begin to operate long before formal education sets in. Existing inequalities in society are pervasive and they do not vanish on their own. The acerbic political and legal fights about positive discrimination in the USA demonstrate how extremely difficult it has become to alleviate what is felt to be injustice by well-intentioned, but in the end defeated policies.

This does not mean we should give up the efforts to increase awareness of the unconscious bias we all have and to combat stereotypes that are built already into the toys that girls and boys are given by parents, whose choice is influenced by their own economic resources and cultural biases, advertisements, toymakers, and the societal expectation of the future roles their children will occupy.[3] In school, the expectation of teachers can exert a big influence, for instance, when girls are made to understand that mathematics is not for them, which later plays out in the differentiation of choosing between the so-called "hard" and "soft" sciences at universities. Even for occupational choices, a heavily skewed distribution is observed in OECD (Organisation for Economic Co-operation and Development) countries, which partly accounts for the persistent gender pay gap.

Which brings us to the one major stumbling block that looms large on the road towards equality of women in science. When career and family obligations overlap, leading to an intense competition

---

3 See Sabine Frühstück, *Playing War: Children and the Paradoxes of Modern Militarism in Japan* (2017) and *Gender and Sexuality in Modern Japan* (2022). One of my former students, Sabine is now Distinguished Professor and the Koichi Takashima Chair in Japanese Cultural Studies in the Department of East Asian Languages & Cultural Studies at the University of California, Santa Barbara.

between opposing demands, especially during the crucial years which are decisive for the choices made and for the future career path, women in science are at a clear disadvantage. I remember discussing these and related gender issues with Rose Laub Coser, an eminent sociologist of medicine and of the family. Together with her husband, the couple has written about "greedy institutions," a term that intuitively appeals to our understanding. Lewis Coser defined it as "institutions that seek exclusive and undivided loyalty and...attempt to reduce the claims of competing roles and status position" (Coser 1974). For him, greedy institutions were those in the public domain, while Rose was concerned with how the greedy institution of the family restricts the participation of women in public life (Coser 1974).

Science, undoubtedly, is a greedy institution, and so is the family. Both demand exclusive and undivided loyalty, but more than that, they are greedy of the time to be devoted exclusively to each of them. Scientific work is not just about long hours and weekends, something it shares with other greedy jobs in the corporate world or in finance, albeit without the generous pay in these sectors. Claudia Goldin, the winner of the 2023 Nobel memorial prize in economics, has analyzed the role of "greedy jobs" on career and family, telling us how to fight inequality and unfairness and how this might lead to better and more productive working lives for all (Goldin 2021).

Once, I wrote a contribution for a collection of essays comparing the situation of women in different countries with the title: "Power Is, Where Women Are Not." The editors removed the title and replaced it with a more innocuous one, although the historical record is clear: when more women move into a profession, it is likely that its status in society is in decline (Nowotny 1981). This is a correlation, not a causal link, but it summarizes the struggles that women continue to be engaged in, demanding recognition, and fighting for equality. Power pervades every single layer of society, as well as the nooks and crannies of daily life. It shapes social hierarchies, be they more flat like the ones in liberal democracies, or impenetrable and backed by force, like in authoritarian regimes. Power relations affect the leadership culture in every organization. Not surprisingly, the power structures that prevail in society cannot be isolated and prevented from seeping into science. There, a normative contradiction emerges.

One of the foundations of the scientific ethos is the norm of scientific universalism. It holds that all scientists' claims should be subjected to the same preestablished impersonal criteria, and that scientific validity is independent of the personal attributes of the protagonists, i.e., regardless of their origin, nationality, ethnicity, and gender (Merton 1973). Scientists espouse universalism. They firmly believe that scientific talent exists everywhere. Every child, as Alison Gopnik observed in her experiments, is born full of curiosity, it is a "scientist in the crib" (Gopnik, Meltzoff, and Kuhl 1999). But it is also obvious—and here the contradiction sets in—that a talented young mind must be nurtured and the road to become a scientist is long and often hard. When it comes to academic positions and especially to the ardently aspired tenured professorship, a buyer's market dominates, as every anxious postdoc in the Western world soon realizes. Every talent, be it scientific, artistic, entrepreneurial, or sportive, is subject to the various selection processes and social filters that operate in accordance with the power structure and values in each sector and in every society. Although Western societies pride themselves to be meritocracies, critics point to the many distortions that arise from the ways in which well-educated and well-earning parents tilt the system to unjustly favor their children. The Matthew Principle in science, according to which advantages tend to accumulate for those who already have them, begins to operate already in the educational system.

Science claims a special place and yet finds itself in a double bind. One reason is the inner normative contradiction between universalism —making no allowance for differences—and the particularism that arises from working with real people, in real situations in different national and cultural contexts, reflecting the local particularities of institutional practices. This makes it so difficult to carve out exemptions, as these must be subjugated again under the claim of being valid for all. It has taken long for women to find their position and voice in science. In previous times, their entry into science depended on the family ties to a man—being a daughter, wife, or sister. Today, women can pursue any career in science independently—and yet, social, and emotional support remain vital. Whenever I am asked by young women scientists what advice I could give them about how to succeed in realizing the aspirations and visions that attracted them to science, my answer is rather simple. First, find out what you really want to do and whether the working conditions you find will allow you to do so. If not, either change what you want to do, or change the conditions. The second part of my advice is even more simple: choose your partner well.

Digression 2

Occasionally I am asked about my work-life balance, a question I find difficult to answer. I consider myself to be among the privileged for whom what they do—work—is an integral part of their life and life without it would be greatly reduced in its meaning and the richness of discoveries it brings. I am immensely grateful for it but realize that many struggle to establish a feasible and meaningful relationship between those parts of their life that have become separated. If "life" is experienced as being self-determined, even if this is partly an illusion, while "work" is permeated by temporal constraints and obligations imposed from outside, attempts to "balance" become rather difficult. This is not to deny that it makes sense to alternate between work and what used to be called leisure; between strenuous efforts and relaxation or even regeneration; between drudgery and excitement; between intensity of efforts and just letting go. To the contrary, these are salutary and necessary practices. But the initial and internalized split of "work" from "life" makes it difficult to reconcile them by searching for a balance.

What matters most for me is the balance between mind and body. Together they constitute the self and, despite the dualism of René Descartes, ideally form a unity through their multiple interactions that pervade cognitive and motor activities, perception and memory, emotion and language. For me, a very simple, basic physiological fact sums it up neatly: I need eight hours of sleep. Without it, my mind does not function the way it should. Whenever, due to circumstances, I try to do with less, I immediately notice a reduction of my cognitive faculties, which further decreases my sense of well-being. Thus, I have learned to yield to my body's needs. I have gained an intuitive understanding what cognitive scientists mean when they speak about "embodied cognition."[4]

The balance between mind-body extends beyond sleep. It includes the urge to move and to gain an awareness of my bodily presence in the environment in which I find myself. This can be outdoors, like

---

4 The concept suggest that many features of cognition are shaped by the physical state and capacities of the organism and the bodily interactions with the situatedness in the environment in which it finds itself. The assumptions about the world are built into the functional structure of brain and body, with the mind emerging from their interactions.

climbing trees as a child, crossing a lake while swimming, hiking in the mountains and, a while ago, rock climbing. I have also developed a somewhat weird habit. Whenever I am in a new place, I want to get to the highest elevation so that I can have an overview of the surroundings to know where I am. Indoors, I intuitively observe my position in the space surrounding me. This may be a socially arranged space, be it in relation to other people or the built environment in which people move or occupy a place assigned to them by formal or informal rules. The mind observes and seeks to map what happens outside its inside representation. It negotiates with the body a position comfortable for both.

It may also happen that the mind signals danger. During the last year of high school, I joined a gliders club with a group of friends. We did not have to build the plane ourselves, but to send one of us into the air was a team effort to be carefully orchestrated under the supervision of an experienced instructor. In those days, a wrench was used to pull up the plane with a steel cable, which at a given height had to be released at the right moment. With the instructor sitting in the plane behind, one learns when exactly the moment has arrived and to do so. Then comes the day which every novice anticipates with joy and much anxiety: the moment when you are completely on your own, sitting in a flying machine without a motor, the wrench pulling you up to the exact height in which you must release the cable—and then you glide, you find the thermal upwind near-by and up you go—feeling an intense sense of freedom filled with the trusted reliance on plane, body, and mind.

It may have been experiences like this that have contributed to my sense of balancing periods of intense work with allowing myself to take a break. I know when I need to have a longer time of rest and have always found ways of making it possible. I cherish my summer vacations and refuse to take on additional obligations, even if they include invitations to participate in otherwise tempting conferences in exotic places or with interesting people. It is important for me to make pauses, a deliberate way of stopping before beginning anew. This allows for looking back as well as forward, for taking stock, however briefly and assessing where one stands before moving on. It is like conscious breathing, inhaling, and exhaling, finding a rhythm that is fundamental for every living organism.

Perhaps this sense for the balance between mind and body deepens my temporal consciousness, the feeling for time, its rhythms and change, but it may also be the other way around. A long time ago, I had one of those rare lucid dreams in which the unconscious mind finds a way to communicate with the conscious mind. It cannot use language, as we dream in images and not in words, but we are able to translate the images into words. In the dream, I saw a photograph of myself that looked like a photograph for a passport. Then, the photograph started to move, and I watched with amazement how my face changed as I became older. Today, this kind of morphing can be performed by an AI, which predicts what we will look like in the future, but in my dream, I was ahead of the time. When the movement stopped, a date appeared below my photograph, and I knew this was the date of my death. I was shocked, but I also realized that a possibility existed to appeal the date of death. All I had to do was to deposit my complaint to the Office of Foretold Death, so I decided to appeal. Then I woke up and took another decision. I would immediately erase the year of my death from my memory and only remember day and month.

Apparently, my appeal was favorably received, as the indicated year of my death, even if I erased it from memory, was in the last century. The remarkable circumstances of this dream were that there were none. Neither was I ill or under stress, nor those close to me. But thinking about death is inevitable as one becomes older, even if my doctor assures me that I have what he calls "good genes." I hope I can maintain the balance between mind and body in the sense that neither the mind, nor the body, gives up before the other. Then, I hope to be ready to be taken by the thermal upwind into another world—into the freedom of the unknown or of nothingness.

IV.

Eigenzeit

My book *Eigenzeit*[1] was published in the memorable year 1989 which, as I have since learned, had very different meanings for different parts of the world and obviously also for each of us.[2] I still regard it as a very personal book whose writing followed the temporal rhythm of my life at the time. I was aiming at a diagnosis of the social and technological changes I observed and how these affected the meaning of the concept of time, of different kinds of exposure to and different experiences of time, all based on social science research while reading, as well as what the natural sciences, from chronobiology to physics, had to offer. I was eager to grasp the plurality of time and its multidimensionality. I was interested in the conflicts that emerged from the experience of time and that make us realize the many tacit assumptions of what we take

---

1 Editor's note: *Eigenzeit* means "time of one's own" (Nowotny 1994).

2 Helga Nowotny, *Eigenzeit: Entstehung und Strukturierung eines Zeitgefühls* (Frankfurt am Main: Suhrkamp Verlag, 1989).

for granted otherwise. I observed how the boundaries between private and public time began to blur in everyday life and became fascinated by the gradual absorption of the notion of the future by what I called the extended present.

Everywhere I looked, I stumbled upon technologies that alter the perception, and experience of time in the most immediate and visible, as well as in an invisible way. These had been the clocks and other time measurement devices with the decisive influence they had on the structuration of time imposed by society, beginning with industrialization, and lasting trough modernity. They were now partly replaced or complemented by the new information and communication technologies. In *Eigenzeit* I set out to retrace the qualitative changes they induced in the individual perception of time and in the corresponding experience through societal time-structuring. I delved into what I called chronopolitics, evident in the many conflicts that make us realize how time is involved in all human interactions and in the political struggles we are engaged in.

My first reflexive encounter with time, as mentioned before, took place when I found myself in Cambridge experiencing an abrupt transition from one temporal regime—having little to no time for myself—to its opposite—an affluence of time which I experienced as pure luxury. I absorbed whatever I could read about social time. By chance, I discovered the existence of the International Society for the Study of Time, ISST, and that its next conference would be held in July 1973 in Japan. The members of ISST came from a wide range of academic disciplines and the great, in fact the only topic they had in common, was time in its fascinating and interdisciplinary multitude. I submitted a paper which was accepted and set off to Lake Yamanaka at the foot of Mt. Fuji. In keeping with my budget, I used the Trans-Siberian Railway and later an East German freighter that took a few passengers on board. On the borrowed typewriter of the captain, I made the final revisions of my paper, which was well received by the conference participants. Time has stayed with me ever since. I kept in contact with ISST, served as its President in the years 1992–1995 and cherished the friendship with J.T. Fraser, the charismatic founder of ISST, and his deep philosophical insights until his death.

In 2016, I was invited by Bernd Scherer to speak in Berlin at a conference on "Time of the Algorithms," a prescient topic on the occasion of celebrating "100 years of the Present" (Scherer 2016). Under the title *Eigenzeit. Revisited* I spoke about my previous work and the changes that had taken place since, especially the developments launched by the latest scientific-technological developments. They included a frenzy of acceleration and the expectation that only more and faster innovation would bring the solution to humanity's visibly growing problems, beginning with climate change and the deterioration of the natural environment. Given the lack of determined action, was humanity running out of time? I spoke about the growing influence of social media, which induces the kind of hyper-fragmentation of temporal experience we have all become familiar with, and the effects that instant communication exert on constituting a medial self, and how this might change the self's embedding in its body and the body's lifetime. I returned to the topic of the future getting absorbed in the present and the advent of big data (Nowotny 2017).

Speaking about time, it is worth recalling the event that almost brought the entire world to a complete standstill when the COVID-19 pandemic hit. Governments were unprepared and reacted in often chaotic ways; panic broke out when hospitals were at the brink of functioning and mortality figures rose; and scientists rushed to high-through sequencing to find out more about the unknown virus before they succeeded in record time to develop a new kind of vaccine based on mRNA (Nowotny 2021a). However, what most of us remember are the lockdown periods of variable lengths and the harsh restrictions of mobility and of social contacts they brought. Inevitably, some of us were gravely affected by these constraints while others were able to accommodate and even profit from them. But for all, a kind of social a-temporality was imposed upon us, resulting in a temporal amnesia that is vaguely referred to as "before" and "after" the pandemic. I remember vividly the day before my first lockdown. Unaware of what was to come, I delivered the Wittrock Lecture at the Swedish Collegium for Advanced Study in Uppsala, devoted to the topic of "Life in the Digital Time Machine" (Nowotny 2020). Later, I succeeded to make good use of the various lockdowns that followed to put the lecture into writing. It adumbrates many of the themes elaborated in my book *In AI We Trust: Power, Illusion and Control of Predictive Algorithms* (Nowotny 2021b). Despite the inconveniences, limitations, and frustrations that the pandemic also held for me, I am deeply grateful for the free time it gave me.

In September 2023 the Kunsthaus Zürich, one of the major museums in the German-speaking world, opened an impressive exhibition on "Zeit" (Time). Cathérine Hug, the curator, retraced the representation and perception of time by combining art, objects and ideas from different epochs in a transhistorical mode, which can also be found in the catalogue (Kunsthaus Zürich 2023). Of the six guiding chapters in the exhibition, one was devoted to *Eigenzeit,* building upon ideas and insights I had written almost forty years earlier. Cathérine invited me for the opening night for a lively discussion on the concept of *Eigenzeit* and what I made of it now. The next morning, I agreed to accompany her on a guided tour through the exhibition that she had arranged for a small group of visitors. As we moved from one space to the next, she spontaneously selected one or two pieces of art and explained the artist's background, intention, and context of the work. Then she turned to me, challenging me to improvise by commenting through the lens of *Eigenzeit* what was before us. The motto of the exhibition, "Live the questions, experience time," took on a special meaning for me as I had to reply immediately.

The exhibition begins with Deep Time. Its time scales exceed by far the power of human imagination. The temporal complexity at work is overwhelming, making it impossible to experience Deep Time directly. At most, we remain in awe and humility for what goes on in the universe and far before and beyond our lifetime. So, where does *Eigenzeit* enter? Where is our place in this multitude of temporal cosmic layers? My answer was to approach *Eigenzeit* through the Anthropocene, which is proposed to mark a new geological epoch in accordance with the rules of the International Union of Geological Sciences, the official gatekeeper of the age of the Earth. If humans have been able to alter the physical layers of Earth, leaving traces of their intervention in the sediments of ancient lakes and radioactive residues in the rocks underground in which nuclear tests were carried out—some of the candidates of a "Golden Spike" which the Anthropocene Working Group must assess—humans have indeed created a new temporal watershed in the chronology of the Earth. The Anthropocene becomes a human made *Eigenzeit* in the context of cosmic Deep Time. It implies to take on the responsibility that is interwoven with human agency. Whatever happens on and with our planet will happen under the temporal regime of humans.

The next room is devoted to Biological Perspectives. The focus is on the dynamics of biological evolution and the biological rhythms, on oscillations and cycles that pulse through and regulate life. Amazing mechanisms of temporal coordination are at work between the regulatory networks of every organism. Without exception, every biological perspective follows the "arrow of time" inscribed in all living organisms, indicating their move from birth to death. One aspect of *Eigenzeit* pertains to the differences in lifespan that living organisms display. The human lifespan is located on a continuum, let us say somewhere between a fruit fly, whose lifespan lasts a few days, and that of elephants or mammals like whales that surpass the human lifespan by many years. In the last 150 years, human longevity has increased significantly, raising expectations even further. Yet, our biological *Eigenzeit* is still determined by the evolutionary heritage and the temporal limitations it imposes. We should treasure it and the insight it conveys. Limits pose constraints, but constraints also spur creativity to make the most of the timespan we have been given. This goes against the fantasies of a transhumanism, rekindled by AI and some of its proponents, who pin their hope on computational artefacts that will allow humans to overcome the defects of living organisms and to defy death. But it is just that: a fantasy, springing from the old human desire to escape death. Biological *Eigenzeit* ground us in the reality of all living organisms.

The next room contains artefacts and images assembled under the theme of Measurable Economic Perspectives. It is filled with exquisite clocks and watches and their artful as well as artistic history, which is still in the making. After all, we are in Switzerland, the homeland of watches with its rich tradition, technological sophistication, and the remarkable ability to restructure its watch industry. Almost nostalgically, the exhibition looks back to the bygone age of industrialization when clocks reigned supreme, displaying the enormous impact they had on people's work and life while extending their global temporal grip through the maximization of efficiency, measurement, and productivity gains. I felt surrounded by *Eigenzeit.* It was palpable in the temporal dialectics materialized and symbolized in the clocks and watches that coordinated, controlled, and imposed linear clock time's rise to power, while at the same time individuals appropriated time and began to fight for their *Eigenzeit*. The fight is far from over, as remote working, the search for work-life balance, and the looming prospect of algorithmic automation show. If AI indeed replaces many middle-class jobs, clock time will yield to digital time. Life in the digital time machine has already begun.

The rest is quickly told. The exhibition takes us next on the information highway. An impressive photograph by Andreas Gursky captures the frenzy of high frequency trading. The action by people on the trading floor has been taken over by algorithms that now define the stock exchange. The *Eigenzeit* of money and the temporal logic of financial markets unite and make the viewer wonder whether these are the forebodings of a world where even more action will be carried out by artificial entities. Next comes the display of the temporal functionality of mass media and social media. In its name, TikTok is a playful reminder of the mechanic movements of a clock. In practice, it generates the experience of time that has become hyper-fragmented. Maybe this signals *Eigenzeit* at the brink, marking a temporal edge where we experiment with time that can still be shared with others; time that remains for ourselves; and full submission to digital time controlled by digital artifacts and those behind them.

I left the exhibition in high spirits. Once more, it confirmed what only art can do when we engage with it. Artists express an intimate and often very personal struggle with something that is of overwhelming importance and relevance for them. It can be a problem of function and form, how to translate an insight or an idea into the materiality and contextuality that is built into artistic practice, while moving forward towards what has not been seen and not been done as yet. Science has its own methods and instrumentation to tackle well-defined scientific problems. It continues to refine and enhance them, with truly amazing achievements. Compared to science, art has many more degrees of freedom. Its indeterminacy is greater, which renders it futile to look for progress of any kind. While science seeks to give answers, art raises more questions.

It is this indeterminacy that creates a greater openness of art in its engagement with the public. Art contains the power that resides in the initial spark, the creative pulse that pushes forward in directions not yet known. A work of art incorporates the question that the artist had. And from time to time, the spark jumps over. It kindles a new insight in others who respond by taking it up and carrying further. This is the meaning of "it struck me" and this is what happened to me when I left the exhibition. I had received a new insight. It confirmed what I had told Anna Elsner in an interview for the catalogue: Yes, Time won't let go of me.

V.

In AI We Trust and the Illusion of Control

My book *In AI We Trust: Power, Illusion and Control of Predictive Algorithms* was published in 2021. Translations into other languages were quick to follow, to my delight with very different cover illustrations. During my journey through what I call "digi-land" I was largely disappointed by the existing literature. Much of it was superficial and ahistorical, pushing a specific and narrow agenda and full of speculation. It seemed that the discussion to catch up with the dynamics of this rapidly developing field and to gauge at least some of the likely major cultural and societal impact got stuck between a limitless techno-optimism on one hand and, on the other, an equally dystopian view with apocalyptic undertones. I had to find a way between these irreconcilable dichotomies, and this was one of the reasons why I focused on predictive algorithms.

Together with the enormous amount of data available and the unprecedented computational power, predictive algorithms change our perception and experience of time. An impressive array of digital technologies gives us access to the past, from the most distant universe and across unimaginable time scales. Paleo-genomics and a treasure of new archeological material, including residues of food that people ate and other data from the human past, are brought into the present. This flood of information works in non-linear ways to open new horizons of understanding and meanings. Simultaneously, the present becomes ever more compressed and overloaded by the hyper-fragmented temporal bits into which we divide our perception and awareness of time, mediated by the digital devices that surround us. Even greater are the changes in the ways how we conceive of the future. Prediction has the power to make the future disappear. The openness of the future is at risk when we believe we can control it through the predictive tools that are increasingly built into decision-making mechanisms and act accordingly. To the extent that we rely on predictive algorithms in the illusion that they are already the future—forgetting that algorithmic predictions are based on data extrapolated from the past and are always couched in probabilities—we let them control us. Paradoxically, the power that predictive algorithms have to make us act in ways they predict reduces our agency over the future.

Then, ChatGPT arrived and took the world by surprise. Even experts were amazed by the feats of Large Language Models (LLMs) to generate texts, images and sounds trained with data taken from the web and even synthetically produced data. The frenzy that erupted has barely abated. Like during the COVID-19 pandemic, it was easy to become an "AI expert" overnight by being drawn into the discussion. I saw academics fall again into the trap that media overexposure holds, assuming scientific authority while propagating their opinion. Only this time, also the media-savvy CEOs of the large corporations threw their weight into the ring, with the clear aim to influence public opinion, while launching massively financed lobbying activities to avoid regulation by government not in their favor. This has rendered scientific communication even more difficult as speculation about what might happen become assertions of what will happen.

New opportunities are celebrated, but also many concerns are raised. They range from threats to undermine liberal democracies through targeted "disinformation" to how to cope with job losses for professionals and artists and the potential benefits and upheavals the diffusion of Generative AI will cause in the health care and education systems. One concern, however, looms large: are humans still in control of AI technologies? This is not about the "existential risk" of an Artificial General Intelligence (AGI) wiping out human agency sometime in the future, a prospect that is conjured only to divert us from attending to problems in the present. Rather, it taps into a deep-seated fear of losing control. Questions arise whether we "overdelegate" when increasingly installing command and control systems into the decision-making structure of public institutions, as well as into businesses. Given the enormous concentration of economic power in a handful of large international corporations and the difficulties that governments experience in regulating AI, is control of this technology handed over to Big Tech? And, given the rise of geopolitical tensions, will it be possible to reach at least minimum regulatory standards at international level or will AI escape control?

I did my modest share in communicating, giving interviews, and interacting, apart from the usual suspects and academic lectures, with audiences as diverse as a class of lower-tier high school students in Italy, the staff of a theater in Germany, trade union representatives in Brussels and an exhibition audience in Barcelona. I continue to be engaged in the Digital Humanism initiative, which started with a Manifesto in 2019 at the Technical University of Vienna.[1] Apart from

1 "Vienna Manifesto on Digital Humanism," DIGHUM, https://caiml.dbai.tuwien.ac.at/dighum/dighum-manifesto.

a regular online Digital Lecture series, most recently an open access textbook has been made available as well (Werthner et al. 2024). Similar initiatives are emerging in other countries. Digital humanism stands for the development of human-centered AI and that AI must become a public good.

An interesting invitation issued in pre-ChatGPT times reached me from the Royal Flemish Academy of Belgium for Sciences and the Arts in Brussels under their innovative "thinker in residence" program. It involved an intense and inspiring round of discussion with members of the academy, reaching out to various groups of stakeholders, and writing a report that, together with the position paper by the academy, includes recommendations addressed to government officials. The theme of "AI as an Agent of Chance" allowed me to widen the perspective and to put AI into a larger picture of humanity's outsourcing of knowledge operations, beginning with the invention of writing and followed by the enormous impact the printing press had. The focus of my recommendations were important policy concerns: launching a broad public campaign under the motto of "AI for citizens—citizens for AI" that aims to support citizens to appropriate and use AI for their benefit and a better society; making basic research in AI a high research priority to counteract the dominance of a one-dimensional "technological solutionism" that ignores or sidelines alternatives in the choice of research problems, methods, and techniques, and vigorous support of research on the impact AI has on society regarding aspects and areas unlikely to be taken up by large international corporations (Nowotny, Van Hoyweghen, and Vandewalle 2023).

Encouraged by a conference in Stockholm where I presented a paper on "AI and the Illusion of Control," I will pursue this theme further (Nowotny 2024). Technology is about control, the ultimate test of every technology to make sure "it works!" A technology is designed, built, and operates according to the functions and goals inscribed in it. As a smooth functioning can never be completely assured, control implies to foresee and prevent what can go wrong. Maintenance, repair, and error control are well-established parts of engineering. Historically, the control of technology could not content itself with its mere technical functioning. The pressure from society grew to extend it far beyond, first by responding to the necessity to guarantee the safety and health of the workers who operated it. Gradually, control was expanded over the conditions under which a technology operates and the impact it produces in the wider context. Control now includes an increasing spectrum of the impacts it has on health and the environment resulting from production processes, products and waste disposal that arise all along. This covers the extraction of minerals and materials needed for production, CO2 emissions, possible toxicity, recycling and more. The requirements to control technology have grown in line with its effectiveness, although a huge gap persists between what is being done compared and what should be done.

Control of technology is never about technology alone. It exerts power by installing constraints on things and processes, prescribing how to interact with them. It also confers power to those who are behind these controls, be it governments or corporations. AI is a technology unlike others, as it aims to reach the level of human cognitive capabilities. Hence the fear of digital surveillance, the concern about fake news and the erosion of trust when hate speech and conspiracy theories circulate unchecked through the social media. The regulation of AI as a technology has barely begun and we are far from understanding the more long-term impact and potential social harm that might come with it if it remains uncontrolled. But there is also the other side of control—the illusion of being in control. Humans are always at risk of being overwhelmed by their senses and biases as well as by overconfidence and sheer hubris. Illusions are nurtured by the cognitive biases we all have, reinforced by social and economic circumstances and by the institutions and cultures into which we are socialized. One peculiar feature of illusion is that those in its grip fail to notice until a clash with reality forces them to do so.

Generative AI, such as ChatGPT and its co-species, have exposed human vulnerability to anthropomorphism, which makes us see things, phenomena, and other entities as more human-like than they really are (Dennett 1989). By mimicking human language and other cognitive and even emotional abilities, the line between the "natural" tendency to anthropomorphize as expressed in the language we use and the belief that the technological artifact is an entity that "knows," "understands" and "thinks," can easily transform into a compelling illusion of being in the presence of a thinking creature like ourselves. The illusion of control over AI technologies is especially tricky as it can lure us into believing that we are dealing with another human being, while we should be aware that the AI system has been designed explicitly to do so. We should heed what Richard Feynman, the physicist, reminds us of: "Science is what we have learned about how to keep from fooling ourselves." The potential of AI technologies is enormous. Learning how to keep from fooling ourselves is only the beginning. Trying to understand how much control and of which kind we will need in a future shaped by the intricate interactions between humans and the technologies created by them must follow.

In the end, human agency must come to terms with the agency that is designed into the machines, while raising awareness about the differences and similarities between human and non-human intelligence. A growing awareness is under way to rethink what is meant by "intelligence," beginning by positioning human intelligence on a spectrum of intelligence inherent in all living organisms. The process of redefining and reasserting human agency must be done in view of the inherent openness of the future. We do not know where the co-evolutionary path on which humans and the machines created by them will lead, nor whether or when something like AGI will be attained. Before reaching such a presumed endpoint, much needs to be done. Also, in this sense, the future is now. It remains uncertain but open.

VI.

What is Next? The Socioscope

The next paths into the future are often connected in unexpected ways with the past. Now, as The Chinese University of Hong Kong Press convinced me to write this memoir after having translated my book *In AI We Trust* into Chinese, I am reminded of my earlier encounters with science in Asia. It was in the early 2000s when I was part of a delegation of the Max Planck Society visiting Shanghai. The occasion was the opening of a small Institute for Advanced Study (IAS); probably I had been invited given my familiarity with this kind of scientific institution. Two episodes from this visit remain in my memory. The German director of the IAS was a big fan and connoisseur of Chinese modern art and introduced us to an artist, whose paintings were already on display on the premises of the IAS, while the last preparations for the opening were still underway. It was yet another tribute for the strong connections between art and science regardless of time and place. The other event was a small, informal colloquium we had with a member of the Chinese Academy of Sciences (CAS). He had just returned from Beijing and explained to us the ambitious plans of the Chinese government to significantly raise the number of top universities in China in the coming years which would be able to compete at the highest international level.

I was often reminded of this announcement when subsequent developments of the international rise of science in China surpassed what we could imagine back then. It is evident in the number of scientific publications, including the percentage of those being highly cited, as well as in the informal impressions gathered by visiting European scientists who spoke highly of the quality of students and researchers they had met. My subsequent brief visits to China were linked to my function as president of the European Research Council, including a talk I gave at the CAS. To my surprise, the director of the Institute of Science Policy presented me with the Chinese edition of our book on Mode 2. I was struck then—as happened several times since by the asymmetry of information—how much more our Asian interlocutors knew about us than we knew about them. In times of rising geopolitical tensions, it is more important than ever to keep communication channels between scientists open. This goes beyond the call for science diplomacy that resurges every time a crisis threatens the existing informal research cooperation across national borders. Science has the power to connect what politics can easily separate. Communication between scientists is essential for science to flourish, and while politics is characterized by ups and downs in international relationships, science is based on a steadfast, yet dynamic long-term perspective.

Next came my first official visit to Singapore, which was related to my functions as ERC president. It included a stop at Nanyang Technological University as I had known Bertil Andersson, the charismatic president of NTU, for many years. He introduced me to Alan Chan, the Dean of the

College of Humanities, Arts, and Social Sciences. Alan spontaneously invited me to return as Visiting Professor once my function with the ERC had come to an end. I had no longer thought about it when a formal invitation arrived somewhat later. I had been impressed by NTU's spectacular rise as a young Asian university and was curious to immerse myself into academic life beyond the Western universities I knew. As I had other obligations as well, I limited my stay to six weeks every year, preferably and understandably during the dark and cold European winters.

Apart from giving a few selected public lectures, my main obligation consisted in interacting and supporting the junior faculty in their research. This turned out to be an excellent opportunity for me to learn much about Singapore seen through the eyes of young researchers. They taught me how they viewed their society and what their aspirations for the future were. Most of the funding for which they had to compete came from the Ministry of Education and thus I could also observe how the priorities set by the MoE were interpreted by them. Although the scope of the research priorities was ample and with a strong focus on Singaporean society, many young researchers tended to overinterpret them and eagerly sought to fit their projects into the existing call for applications. Later, when I had been asked to advise the recently established Social Science Research Council, I argued to leave sufficient space for bottom-up ideas, as cultivating scientific independence among young talents is the precondition for science to advance. These are the "white" calls in official funding agency parlance, while in Europe we speak about "blue-sky" research. Although the overwhelming focus of research in Singapore is on applied research with a strong, pragmatic bend, for reasons that have much to do with Singapore's history as a young and future-oriented nation, I remain convinced that every society with high technological potential and ambition is well advised to carve out a space for fundamental research that has proven to be the breeding ground for the "usefulness of useless knowledge."

Nowhere did I encounter so much serious attention devoted to the future as in Singapore. Foresight reports and a multitude of analyses continue to proliferate. They are pervasive in official government documents and in policy discourse, as much as is the preoccupation with the future in the minds of citizens. It takes many forms. Singaporean society has early adopted life with digital devices. They play an important role in communication, but also in shaping a future-oriented outlook. From apps that record continuously updated measurements of pollution to detailed warnings about potential hazards of other kinds, from convenience apps that offer choices to consumers to receiving messages from the government, digital devices are consulted continuously to guide behavior, prevent harm, and optimize future well-being. Interspersed with sophisticated incentives designed into policy measures, Singaporean society seems to have fully embraced a digital future shaped by the behavior and attitude of what people do in the present. The narrative of the potential vulnerability of a small city state surrounded by big and powerful neighbors has been fully adopted. Instead of what could easily have turned into a pessimistic vision, a robust self-confidence rules, infused with techno-optimism, yet always with an underlying warning to protect the assets people benefit from at present. Sustained and boosted by the comparatively high trust that the government enjoys and legitimated by what it can deliver on its promises, I became fascinated by the many ingenious incentive structures built into governmental policies.

The COVID-19 pandemic did not halt before Singapore and my annual visits stopped as well. Many studies have since come forth comparing the impact and effectiveness of the various measures that governments deployed at different points in time to cope with the unexpected. The results are mixed, and the final verdict is still out. Nevertheless, it appears that if the numbers of deaths are taken as the main criteria, and holding other factors constant, the differences in the respective effectiveness of adopted policy measures are quite small (Burg and Ausubel 2023). What is much more difficult to assess are the differences in impact the pandemic had on individuals and specific groups. Singapore had an extremely restrictive policy of letting people cross borders, which also affected the universities. While foreign faculty members could leave, they no longer could return, which led to a substantial loss in some university departments. But it would not be Singapore, if the pandemic would not also have had a major impact on thinking about future emergencies, especially pertaining to food security. As the country is highly dependent on food imports, it was decided to raise the degree of food autonomy in Singapore to 30% of the total food supply by 2030. I have no doubt that this aim will be achieved and my work on the Socioscope project may allow me to find out how it is being done.

Which leads me to the next research project I will be engaged in. During the COVID-19 pandemic I was involved in efforts led by Saadi Lahlou, Director of the Institut d'études avancées de Paris, an Institute for Advanced Study, to create a digital platform hosting social science research projects on the pandemic. It offered participants global visibility to share their ongoing research, and to connect with others. At its peak, the platform hosted more than 1,000 projects, many from the Global South and open in eleven languages, leveraging a cloud architecture to make it user-friendly and reactive.[1] After the end of the pandemic, Saadi and I discussed possible other uses of the technical

1 World Pandemic Research Network (WPRN), https://wprn.org.

infrastructure and the ideas behind it. Eventually, we converged on a set of scientific questions we share and deeply care about which amounts to: how do societal transitions towards greater sustainability happen?

Transformation is one of the Big Questions in the social sciences. It underlies political discourse and strategies aiming for major societal, economic, and technological change in desirable directions, like the EU's green and digital transition. It is ubiquitous in many research programs and drives the agenda of the rapidly growing field of sustainability transitions (Koehler et al. 2019). Adopting a multi-level perspective, scenario-based and other techniques, it seeks to bridge the gap between case studies at the microlevel and the models that depict what happens at the societal macrolevel. Despite the impressive amount of theoretical and empirical-methodological evidence accumulated so far by an emerging "transition science," we were not entirely satisfied with the results obtained so far. As mentioned before, many case studies are too small and much too scattered in space and time to allow for meaningful comparison, and many of the dazzling theoretical concepts are too abstract and devoid of empirical evidence to derive understanding for the underlying processes driving a transition.

In Saadi, I found a research partner with complementary experience and skills yet sharing the will to explore and to take risks, even if it means to go against dominant paradigms. We were keen to use the already existing digital infrastructure to develop a new instrument that would give us access to observe, monitor, and follow in real time clusters of local initiatives that are moving in the direction of greater sustainability. We want to explore the motivation and visions that drive the actors "on the ground" and what exactly it is they are striving to achieve. At the same time, we want to analyze the network structures that emerge around their activities and transactions, how they change over time, and which effect these changes have on the systemic level. We are keen to find out which patterns, or clusters, the local initiatives form, as they are all embedded in various ways in the larger environment through the financial, economic (market and non-market), administrative, political, and socio-cultural transactions they perform. We expect that these transactions often overlap, but which constellations that develop over time and how fast; in various geographical and political places; with which kind of resources and human ingenuity and perseverance; and under which kinds of constraints; are more likely to succeed or fail? And how is success or failure defined?

In short, we are eager to gain new insights into the processes that convert what happens at the microlevel into changes at the macrolevel. Is sustainability only possible if it scales up? As an exemplary system for societal transition, we chose the domain of food production, distribution, and consumption, with a focus on sustainability. Food is ideal to study as a model system as it involves a multitude of different actors that interact in a great variety of ways. The transactions involved range from the cultural significance attributed to food to the place food security occupies among the SDGs (The 17 Sustainable Development Goals of the UN) and global challenges; from traditional food chains to modern market economies and the rapid evolution of food production, distribution, and consumption under the pressure of climate change, reduction of harmful emissions, and changing political and social requirements. However valuable will be what we learn about food transition towards greater sustainability, the hope is that the instrument will find application also in other domains.

In our search for the further development of the instrument, we found an unusually open, generous, and congenial interlocutor in Markus Reinhard, the managing director of the NOMIS Foundation in Switzerland. With his support we were able to refine and rigorously test a prototype of our pioneering methodology across continents. The time we were accorded to do so yielded many rewards. Thus, we found that the use of video in gaining access to local initiatives, and to interview the participants, is highly effective. It creates a communicative space for interviewer and interviewee that easily allows to combine information gained in verbal, visual and auditory ways, as well as including information about the local context. We also offer a short video edited by us after the visit as a token of gratitude to the participants in the study. Uploading the initiative on the platform of the Socioscope offers the opportunity for participants to liaise with others, if they wish to do so. These are only some of the advantages we collected by being able to first build a prototype.

The Socioscope is foremost a new instrument to collect data in novel ways, but one of the foremost aims is to be able to scale up the entire process. By carefully designing, standardizing and calibrating the methodology of the instrument, we will be able to conduct the study in several countries and across continents at roughly the same time and to gain a high and meticulously monitored quality of data. It will allow comparison as well reaching statistical significance of qualitative data. We then intend to deploy the latest state-of-the-art in quantitative, agent-based modeling and network analysis. We have set up close cooperation with the Complexity Science Hub Vienna and its president, Stefan Thurner, one of the world-class leaders in complexity science. In September 2023, the Board of the NOMIS Foundation approved our research project. An exciting new part of my trajectory can start, for me and for all those involved in the project.

The Socioscope project is as highly ambitious as it is risky. It requires a more collaborative and team-based approach to research than usual and presupposes a more demanding role for project management, with strict deadlines and clear-cut division of labor where necessary. To build an instrument must never lose sight of why one wants to do it and what its function will be. We are convinced that such an instrument is needed. Compared to the natural sciences, social science research is held back by the lack of instruments at its disposal. The last innovation took place decades ago and was related to the consolidation and expansion of survey research. The uptake of digital tools opened access to new data, especially data from the Internet and phone communications, but soon met various constraints due to ownership and privacy restrictions as well as being suitable only for a specific set of research questions.

We are not naïve in trusting that "data will speak for themselves" nor that an instrument can function without theoretical assumptions of what one is looking for. The prototype we have developed has proven to be extremely valuable in letting us see what we now have to explore at scale—the diversity that exists among the local initiatives and the clusters they form, as well as uncovering the connections and mechanisms that link the societal micro and macro level. We are excited and hope that the Socioscope will succeed in opening new methodological pathways ahead and allow us to better understand how societal transformation occurs.

Digression 3

I have learned to know when to play by the rules and when to subvert them.

Regarding the future, it is important to know the past, as well as your own, but equally important to be able to leave it behind. I am not a nostalgic person. Looking back, I realize that even the most beautiful moments belong to an irretrievable past. We cannot have them back.

Instead, I look forward and I enjoy planning, not because I believe that things will go according to plan, but simply because it helps me to better organize my daily life. This is short-term planning, while I never made any long-term plans. We should have another word for it.

I also do things that need to be done almost immediately. People are usually surprised and thank me for being so quick, but there is nothing unusual about it. It is just a way to clean the daily agenda and leave room for new things to come which I do not anticipate, nor plan for. It seems paradoxical, but the better organized I am in my daily life, the more flexible I am.

I have never understood the fascination many people have for the "great"—whether they are the "great men" (in those times almost exclusively men), be it in science or sports, in the world of entertainment or culture. When in High School, a group of us liked to go to the Staatsoper of Vienna which offered cheap standing places. Many of my classmates were star-struck by a particular opera singer, while others became fans of a particular movie star or a popular theater actor they adored, and would wait for hours to get a closer glimpse of him or an autograph. I could be in awe about their performance, but never grasped why I should admire a person I did not even know personally.

This makes it difficult for me to answer questions about the role models I had. Of course, I have been influenced by many persons, ideas, books, and events, all my life long. But I never had a role model, nor did I miss it. In High School, we had a wonderful teacher who introduced us to the most recent "modern" literature and trends in culture. We were thrilled every hour we could spend with her. I had a good teacher in mathematics and physics, which is the reason why I liked these subjects, while the teacher in biology was an ignorant disgrace, which considerably lowered my interest until another door opened for wanting to know more about the life sciences.

Such an experience is not unusual, especially during the formative years of adolescence. It also says a lot about how our school system fails us. Each of us remembers the good teachers we had as well as the bad ones, and we knew the difference. Once I conducted a small empirical study interviewing scientists who were on the list of "One Hundred Top Scientists of Austria." Among others, I asked them when and how they knew that they wanted to become a scientist. The answers fell into three, clear-cut groups. There were those who were deeply influenced already at a young age by their father (not one single mother at that time!) or a close (male) relative or friend of the family. This is the group where science runs in the (patrilineal) family. There were those whose interest in science was kindled by a book which literally opened a new world for them that took them in and which they never left. This occurred typically during adolescence. It is a tribute to the power of ideas and underlines the importance of making young people appreciate to read. The third category was initiated into science by a teacher, usually in high school. I do not know whether these teachers were considered a role model. More likely, they were seen as the font of knowledge and ideas, opening for the young, inquisitive mind a gateway to understanding what held the world together. This is probably the oldest way in which knowledge continues to be transmitted.

If I were to repeat the study with a group of bright and already established younger scientists today, the answers would probably add a new category or show more overlaps. The means to access knowledge already at a young age have expanded enormously and will grow even more once the potential of Generative AI and other digital tools will become integrated into the educational system. I presume, however, that it will still take a human to interact with, someone who answers questions and gently guides the inquiry. We will still need devoted teachers and adults, as well as books, podcasts and other pedagogical means to pass on to future generations what we know.

My interest in science was awakened when I was eight years old. I had no idea what science was and nobody to tell me. But I grasped that I wanted to enter this world in which I could discover new phenomena and how to explain them and in which ideas mattered. I wanted to understand how I could learn to understand more of what I observed around me and get answers to the questions that interested me. I did not quite know the way to get there, but it was associated with the world out there, with books and ideas and to continue to ask my questions. Partly, this could be obtained in school, but I was early aware that life outside school had much more to teach us.

The circumstances of kindling my interest in the world of knowledge at this age were specific to time and place. It was after the war and conditions in cities were dire. An initiative was started to bring children from Vienna to the countryside or smaller towns where families volunteered to host and nourish them for three months, as more food was available there than in post-war cities. I was sent to the most Western part of Austria, the province of Vorarlberg, bordering Switzerland. The local dialect is very close to German Swiss and even the mentality to "save, work hard and build a house" is similar. During the first days, I did not understand one word of what was spoken. It could have been Danish or Portuguese for me (these were the European countries that also took in children from Austria after the war). Suddenly, I experienced how my brain switched. From one minute to the next I understood the language and easily followed the conversation. It was an unforgettable moment. It seemed a miracle and I realized that something had occurred in my mind which was a great discovery.

My host family was warm and generous. They had six children; the two youngest boys were my age. The house was always full.

The father and oldest son were the local chimney sweepers and the apprentices who worked with them were living with us. Meals had to be punctually prepared as well as heating the bathhouse in time for them to wash when the day ended. Everything was new for me and exciting, like trying to milk the cow the family owned (difficult), climbing a tree (easy), and transporting a pig across the mountain (challenging). I attended the local school and as the level of schooling in Vienna, despite bombardments and not much time spent in the classroom, was more advanced, the teacher decided to appoint me as his assistant. After school, I would correct the exercises that my classmates had written on the slate that was still in use. Of course, this helped to boost my self-confidence, but also provided an extra opportunity to put questions to the teacher who seemingly enjoyed spending extra time with his new pupil from Vienna.

Like in other families in the countryside, a strict division of labor prevailed between men and women. The mother, the only daughter who was twelve years old and a maid, were responsible for preparing the meals and looking after the kitchen garden, cleaning, and washing for the extended household. The men were working outside and took care of the farming activities that were complementing the core work of chimney sweeping. Everybody worked hard, but to me, women's work seemed much harder. Above all, it never ended. It reinforced my aversion against housework and the father, who was normally rather taciturn, teasingly called me "the born housewife." I do not know whether this explains why I never had a role model. There was much to learn from what I observed around me, but it never converged or took shape in one person to admire and to emulate.

In the end, my stay with the family lasted much longer than foreseen. I wrote a letter to my parents, explaining what a great time I had and telling them that I wanted to stay longer. They agreed but insisted that I return to Vienna in time for the next school year, the last year of elementary school and decisive for being able to enter the Gymnasium.

To this day, I am reluctant and somewhat embarrassed when a younger woman approaches me after a lecture or in a conference, telling me that I am her role model. I understand what she means, but I reply that all she can learn from me is the will to find her own way.

I hope that my memoir will be read in this spirit.

VII.

Epilogue: What Follows?

This is a question I have been asking myself continuously as well as of others. If knowledge is power, as Francis Bacon claimed in the early years of modern science, what follows from it? To which use are we putting what we have discovered, invented, or now understand better? The question is about keeping the creative spark alive, letting it diffuse and take us into different contexts of application. It is about the power of knowledge, but not in the triumphant sense in which it is usually interpreted. Rather, it is a genuine attempt to fully acknowledge how little we know about the unintended consequences of human action and, before human action and beyond it, what we know and how we know. The question seeks also to elucidate how inclusive knowledge is, who shares what kind of knowledge with whom and who benefits from it. It is our responsibility to keep asking the same question again and again—what follows?

Ideally, my wish to know how societal transformations happen will produce useful insights into the mechanisms of how local innovations can succeed to instigate change at the level of the system, if at all, as many will die on the way. But I am convinced that even if we cannot attribute what policymakers like to do with fierce conviction—namely to trace the impact of local action—they contribute to overall change. This is where the network perspective enters, as changes in the network structure bring about change in the system. We might end up understanding better which role the visions play that motivate people and guide their behavior and how the response of institutions in the sense of supporting, rejecting, or sidelining them matters. We will not come up with a formula or recipe for transition management, but hope to identify sensitive intervention points, including their timing. The inner dynamics of complex systems with their unexpected potential for change arising from the structure of the networks that continuously form and unform are far from being predictable. Simulation models enable us to ask "what—if?" and thus expand our imagination of what is possible in a quantitative way.

The question "how?" is an easy question compared to asking "why?," which resonates with us as an essential part of the human condition. It returns to haunt us, especially in dark times like the ones we are living through right now. The horrific events and the immense suffering that are caused by war and the numerous frozen conflicts in the world that repeatedly flare up in violence cry out, again, for an answer: *why does it happen, why?* This question was raised by Albert Einstein during the inter-war years in his conversation with Sigmund Freud but frustratingly endures (Einstein and Freud 1933). Amid rising geopolitical tensions, especially between the USA and China, it has stayed with us unanswered until this day, despite the ready explanations offered by strategists and experts of all kinds.

Our view and understanding of the long-term history of humanity is expanded in unprecedented ways by including the latest scientific evidence about the interplay of changes in climate with human history (Frankopan 2023). It offers the opportunity to learn more about how humans coped, or failed, by discovering the patterns that emerge from the cultivation practices in lands that underwent the effects of droughts, volcanic eruptions and jumps in temperature. We know more than ever about the collapse of empires, based on constellations of climate change and imperial overreach, exacerbated by political and economic dysfunctions that wiped out entire civilizations. In retrospect, we can also see the choices that existed at the time, although our ancestors were blind towards them. Uncanny similarities with the present emerge, worsened by the fact that we no longer interpret such changes as evidence of punishment meted out by gods. Instead, the latest findings from scientific-technological advances like ice-core boring, infrared spectroscopy, satellite imaging and the evidence they offer, are right before our eyes.

For the first time also, we now have AI/ML to assist us in identifying, collecting evidence and interpreting what we want to know. AI/ML is already widely used in scientific inquiry and practice. As its capacities are built up, it will become an even stronger asset, which may turn out to be a partner or a rival. If unregulated, we allow it do harm. We may fall into the illusion of control, but we may also use it to learn more about us. AI may help to bring society and its political and economic leaders on the side of science, or it may undermine further the trust that parts of the public have lost in their elites. But we should guard against the temptation of a techno-solutionism. Technology alone is never sufficient. Every technological innovation has to be embedded into a social fabric that consists of organizations, rules and regulations, economic incentives, structures of inequalities and cultural mindsets. Also science has its limitations. As a social institution it is part of the society that supports it, and it will have to continue to negotiate the tension between its claim to universalism and the particularisms that connect it with time and place.

Therefore, I have retrieved the last line of the first haiku I have ever written on AI, which contains an assertion and a plea: *future needs wisdom*. Wisdom entails the ability to render the experience from the past fertile for the present while taking the social and cultural context into account. It means learning to live with ambivalence and to embrace uncertainty. Wisdom knows how to avoid the illusion of control, but it does not give up on holding us responsible for our actions.

References

Burg, David and Jesse H. Ausubel. "Trajectories of COVID-19: A Longitudinal Analysis of Many Nations and Subnational Regions." *PLoS ONE* 18, no. 6 (2023): e0281224. https://doi.org/10.1371/journal.pone.0281224.

Coser, Lewis. *Greedy Institutions. Patterns of Undivided Commitment.* New York: Free Press, 1974.

Dennett, D. C. *The Intentional Stance.* Cambridge, Mass.: The MIT Press, 1989.

Douglas, Mary. *How Institutions Think.* Syracuse: Syracuse University Press, 1986.

Einstein A., Freud, S. (1933 [1932]), "Why War?" In *The Standard Edition of the Complete Psychological Works of Sigmund Freud Vol. 22*, 195–215. London: Hogarth, 1933.

Elliott, Anthony. *Algorithms of Anxiety.* Cambridge: Polity Press, 2024.

Felt, Ulrike. "Knowing and Living in Academic Research." In *Knowing and Living in Academic Research. Convergence and Heterogeneity in Research Cultures in the European Context*, 17–39. Prague: Institute of Sociology of the Academy of Sciences of the Czech Republic, 2009.

———. "The Temporal Fabric of Academic Lives: Of Weaving, Repairing, and Resisting." In *Inquiring into Academic Timescapes*, edited by Filip Vostal, 267–280. Bingley: Emerald Publishing, 2021.

Feyerabend, Paul. *Against Method.* London: New Left Books, 1975.

Flexner, Abraham and Robbert Dijkgraaf. *The Usefulness of Useless Knowledge.* Princeton: Princeton University Press, 2017. https://doi.org/10.2307/j.ctvc77fxf.

Frankopan, Peter. *The Earth Transformed: An Untold History.* New York: Knopf, 2023.

Gibbons, Michael, Camille Limoges, Helga Nowotny, Simon Schwartzman, Peter Scott, and Martin Trow. *The New Production of Knowledge: The Dynamics of Science and Research in Contemporary Societies.* London: Sage Publications, 1994.

Goldin, Claudia. *Career and Family: Women's Century-Long Journey toward Equity.* Princeton: Princeton University Press, 2021.

Gopnik, Alison, Andrew Meltzoff and Patricia Kuhl. *The Scientist in the Crib: What Early Learning Tells Us About the Mind.* New York: William Morris and Company, 1999.

Grossman, Pam, John L. Jackson and Helga Nowotny. "Foreword" and "Afterword." In *Curiosity Studies: A New Ecology of Knowledge*, edited by Perry Zurn and Arjun Shankar. Mineapolis: University of Minnesota Press, 2020. https://doi.org/10.5749/j.ctvzpv67w.

Hausen Karin and Helga Nowotny. *Wie männlich ist die Wissenschaft?* Berlin: Suhrkamp, 1986.

Huber, Andreas and Thomas König. *A History of the Institute for Advanced Studies (IHS) in Vienna Based on Its Key Figures.* Vienna: OSF Preprints, 2023. https://doi.org/10.17605/OSF.IO/7UVQN.

Kahneman, Daniel. *Thinking, Fast and Slow.* New York: Farrar, Straus and Giroux, New York, 2011.

Karikó, Katalin. *Breaking Through: My Life in Science.* London: Penguin, 2024.

Koehler, Jonathan et al. "An Agenda for Sustainability Transitions Research: State of the Art and Future Directions." *Environmental Innovation and Societal Transitions* 31 (June 2019): 1–32. https://doi.org/10.1016/j.eist.2019.01.004.

Kornai, János. *By Force of Thought. Irregular Memoirs of an Intellectual Journey.* Cambridge, Mass.: The MIT Press, 2006.

Krull, Wilhelm and Helga Nowotny. "Decisive Day for European Research." *Science* 306, no. 5698 (Nov 2004): 941. DOI: 10.1126/science.1106368.

Kunsthaus Zürich. "Time. From Dürer to Bonvicini." Exhibition Catalog. Kohn: Snoek, 2023.

Lamont, Michèle. *Seeing Others: How Recognition Works and How It Can Heal a Divided World.* New York: Atria/One Signal Publishers, 2023.

Lonsdale, Sarah. "'I Would Like to Thank My Wife.' An Acknowledgement of Acknowledgements." *Times Literary Supplement.* December 22/29, 2023: 15.

Merton, Robert K. *The Sociology of Science: Theoretical and Empirical Investigations.* Chicago: University of Chicago Press, 1973.

Neiman, Susan. *Left Is Not Woke.* Hoboken: Wiley, 2023.

Nowotny, Helga. *Kernenergie. Gefahr oder Notwendigkeit.* Berlin: Suhrkamp, 1979.

———. "Women in Public Life in Austria." In *Access to Power. Cross-National Studies of Women and Elites (1st ed.)*, edited by Cynthia Fuchs Epstein and Rose Laub Coser. London: Routledge, 1981. https://doi.org/10.4324/9780429423819.

———. *Time: The Modern and Postmodern Experience*, trans. Neville Plaice, Cambridge: Polity Press, 1994.

———. *Es ist so. Es könnte auch anders sein.* Frankfurt am Main: Suhrkamp, 2000.

———. *Insatiable Curiosity: Innovation in a Fragile Future.* Cambridge, Mass: MIT Press, 2008.

———. *The Cunning of Uncertainty.* Cambridge, Mass: Polity Press, 2015.

———. "Eigenzeit, Revisited." In *An Orderly Mess*, edited by Helga Nowotny. Budapest—New York: Central European University Press, 2017.

———. *Life in the Digital Time Machine*. The Wittrock lecture Book Series. No. II. Uppsala: Swedish Collegium for Advanced Study (SCAS), 2020.

———. "In AI We Trust: How the COVID-19 Pandemic Pushes us Deeper into Digitalization." In *Pandemics, Politics, and Society: Critical Perspectives on the Covid-19 Crisis*, edited by Gerard Delanty. Boston: De Gruyter, 2021a. https://doi.org/10.1515/9783110713350.

———. *In AI We Trust: Power, Illusion and Control of Predictive Algorithms*. Cambridge, Mass: Polity Press, 2021b.

———. "The Illusion of Control: Living with Digital Others." *Global Perspectives* 5 (1): 2024. https://doi.org/10.1525/gp.2024.117336.

Nowotny, Helga and Elena Esposito. "Helga Nowotny in Conversation with Elena Esposito." *Sociologica* 16, no. 2 (2022): 261–273. https://doi.org/10.6092/issn.1971-8853/15464

Nowotny, Helga and Ulrike Felt. *After the Breakthrough: The Emergence of High-Temperature Superconductivity as a Research Field*. Cambridge: Cambridge University Press, 1997.

Nowotny, Helga and Pieter Leroy. "Helga Nowotny: An Itinerary between Sociology of Knowledge and Public Debate." Interview by Pieter Leroy. *Natures Sciences Sociétés* 17, no. 1 (Jan–March 2009): 57–64. http://dx.doi.org/10.1051/nss/2009010.

Nowotny, Helga and Giuseppe Testa. *Naked Genes: Reinventing the Human in the Molecular Age*. MA: MIT Press, 2011.

Nowotny, Helga, Ine Van Hoyweghen and Joos Vandewalle. "AI as an Agent of Change—KVAB Thinkers." KVAB Position paper 85 b, 2023.

Nowotny, Helga and Peter Scott. "Mode of Knowledge Production." In *Elgar Encyclopedia of Interdisciplinary and Transdisciplinarity*, edited by Frédéric Darbellay. Cheltenham: Edward Elgar Publishing, 2024.

Pinker, Steven. *Enlightenment Now: The Case for Reason, Science, Humanism, and Progress*. London: Viking, 2018.

Scherer, Bernd. *Die Zeit der Algorithmen*. Berlin: Matthes & Seitz, 2016.

Scott, James C. *Seeing Like a State: How Certain Schemes to Improve the Human Condition Have Failed*. New Haven: Yale University Press, 1998. http://www.jstor.org/stable/j.ctt1nq3vk.

Stern, Sheldon M. *The Cuban Missile Crisis in American Memory.* Stanford: Stanford University Press, 2012.

Turchin, Peter. *End Times: Elites, Counter Elites and the Path of Political Disintegration.* London: Allen Lane, 2023.

Weber, Max. "Wissenschaft als Beruf." In *Geistige Arbeit als Beruf. Vier Vorträge vor dem Freistudentischen Bund.* Munich: Erster Vortrag, 1919.

Werthner, Hannes et al., eds. *Introduction to Digital Humanism. A Textbook.* Springer Nature, 2024. https://link.springer.com/book/10.1007/978-3-031-45304-5.

Ziman, John. "Selling Science." *Nature* 385 (1997): 498–499. https://doi.org/10.1038/385498a0.

Zweig, Stefan. *Die Welt von Gestern. Erinnerungen eines Europäers.* London: Hamish-Hamilton and Stockholdm: Bermann-Fischer Verlag AB, 1942.

1) Helga getting her glider license, 1955.
2) The White House, Washington D.C., 1954. Helga was part of the group of American Field Service students spending one year in the USA. At the end of their stay, they embarked on a bus tour, with an invitation from President Eisenhower to visit the Rose Garden of the White House (Helga is the girl wearing white gloves.).

3) Helga with daughter Katinka in New York City, 1965/66.
4) Helga with daughter Katinka (right), their friend Susumu and their dog Noel, 1973.
5) Helga (far left, seated) with French sociologist Pierre Bourdieu (2nd from right, seated), Villa Serbelloni Bellagio, Italy, 1972.
6) Helga at a conference of the International Society for the Study of Time (ISST) in Japan in 1973 with J. T. Fraser (middle, looks sideways to his right. Helga stands to his left), who was the president of ISST from 1992 to 1995.
7) At the University of Bielefeld, where Helga taught a science and technology studies course, 1980.
8) As Director of the European Center for Social Welfare, and Social Science Research (1974–1987).
9) Helga moderating the Austrian late night discussion show "CLUB 2" (on Austrian TV), 1987.
10) Among men, the Swedish Royal Academy of Sciences, circa 1988–1990.

8.

10.

«Mir ist der Dialog zwischen Natur- und Sozialwissenschaften ein grosses Anliegen.»

Helga Nowotny
Ordentliche Professorin für Wissenschaftsphilosophie und Wissenschaftsforschung
geboren 1937 in Wien

11) In 1992, Helga helped establish the Colle Budapest, a beautiful baroque building lo on top of the hill of Buda, through the initia of Wolf Lepenies and Joachim Nettelbec

12) Inside pages from *Wege in die Wissensch* with the headline "The Next Generation of Female Scientists" (September 1997). The of the little girl is Helga's granddaughter Iso who has just finished her Ph.D. at the Unive Music and Performing Arts in Vienna.

13) With Yehuda Elkana (1st from right), a philosopher and historian of science, École Polytechnique Fédérale de Lausa (EPFL), November 1997.

14) Cover photo of *Das Magazin of the Tages-Anzeiger and Berner Zeitung BZ* (Newspapers in Switzerland), July 13– 1996, during her time at ETH Zurich.

15) Helga at the Swiss Federal Observatory, where the Collegium Helveticum resides, built by German architect Gottfried Semper, 1999.

16) Helga with the renowned Hungarian scientist Edward Teller (carrying a walking stick) at Collegium Budapest (date unknown).

17) Helga with José Manuel Barroso (middle), former president of the European Commission, and Greek biologist Fotis Kafatos (left), July 2007.

18) European Research Council launch conference with former German president Horst Köhler (middle, with orange tie)in Berlin, September 2007.

19) With Spanish King Juan Carlos I (3rd from right, line) with European Research Council, 2010.

20) Helga (center) moderates at Falling Walls Conference 2011, with speakers Mary Kaldc (2nd from right), Nick Barton (2nd from left), Jean-Luc Lehners (1st from right), and Rebecc Cassidy (1st from left).

21) Helga speaking at the World Economic Foru Davos, 2013.

22) Helga was listed among "The Top 50 Women World Business" in the category Technology an Science by the *Financial Times*, 2011.

23) Helga and siniologist Alain Peyraube in Beijing, 2013. Helga was representing the European Research Council at the Annual Meeting of the Champions, hosted by the World Economic Fo

Helga with Pablo Amor, former director of the European Research Council Executive Agency, at her farewell in Brussels in front of the Auditorium Helga Nowotny, 2013.

Helga with the publishing team of the Chinese University of Hong Kong Press, 2024.

The sculpture of Giordano Bruno, a work by Helga's friend Alexander Polzin, depicts an Italian philosopher (1548–1600) who is a heroic figure and a rebel for science. The sculpture represents an act of defiance for her.

A scroll showing the calligraphy of Shiseki Renju (1842–1914), the 44th generation of Ōbaku Monk Nembutsu Dokutan, was purchased by Helga in Paris many years ago. The phrase "洗心養神" means to remove one's miscellaneous thoughts from the mind and rest to attain mental tranquility.

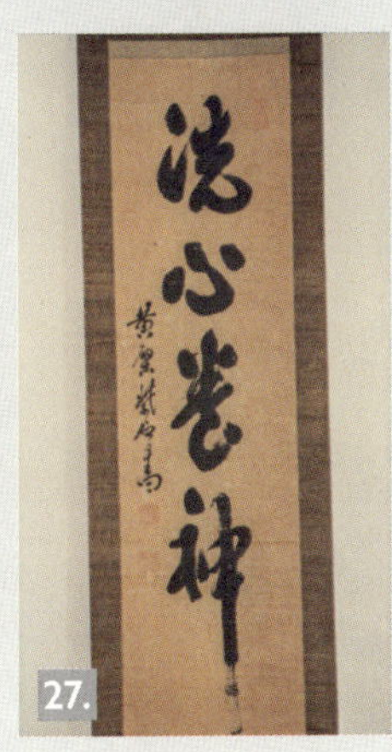

PART TWO

The reason why

we will not lose the future is simple

There is no predetermined future

only a future that is as radically open

as it is inherently uncertain

I

Preface to *The Cunning of Uncertainty*[*]

I have been fortunate to encounter the cunning of uncertainty many times at crucial points in my life. Writing about uncertainty is never about uncertainty alone, and the future remains an ultimate inexhaustible reservoir of uncertainty. The preface invites the reader to follow the cunning of uncertainty, first, as a powerful incentive in the striving for more knowledge. Uncertainty is an inherent part of research and scientists thrive at the cusp of uncertainty. Also, in institutions and organizational life, coping with uncertainty is a constant feature. It necessitates adaptation, anticipation, preparedness and even innovation. Next, I introduce the cunning of uncertainty that often acts as a subversive force of reasoning and action, arriving at unexpected moments. It alerts us to serendipity, to treasure ambiguity, and can be a potent counterforce to false certainties. The more we acknowledge and recognize uncertainty, the less

[*] Originally published in Helga Nowotny, "Preface: It Could Be Otherwise," in *The Cunning of Uncertainty* (Cambridge: Polity Press, 2016), vi–xiv.

we need to feel threatened by it. In the last part, I draw on my professional experience in studying science in the context of society. Science has developed a culture of embracing uncertainty, while society and many politicians crave for certainty, not realizing that learning to cope with uncertainty is one of the most precious cultural resources we have.

This is a book which is dear to my heart. It speaks from personal and professional experience and is based on a firm belief in the human capability of making sense and to create meaning. It allows us to see the contingencies in the world we live in and opens new perspectives on what we know and what we do not know yet, urging us to move on. I wanted my readers to actively engage with the cunning of uncertainty and to embrace it. Unfortunately, the pandemic has shown that what can go wrong, sometimes goes wrong. The uncertainty that came with the unknown virus was not acknowledged. Instead, governments everywhere held on to false certainties and, after an initial short-lived peak, trust in science declined. Widespread confusion gave room to those who denied the efficiency of vaccines, which in many countries was exploited by far-right politicians for their own ends. The many negative fallouts of the pandemic are still with us. The younger generation lost precious years of their lives and is still plagued by anxieties. The economic recovery takes longer than expected. The world before the pandemic is very different from the world after the pandemic. We have not trusted the cunning of uncertainty and were unable to embrace uncertainty.

❐❏❐

The knowledge base means more. It enables greater certainty in orientation and practical intervention when confronted with numerous uncertainties. The rise of modern science and technology has led to the vast improvements of material, living conditions that provide the potential to lift the remaining parts of the world population out of poverty. Our scientific-technological civilization has developed enormous capabilities to anticipate risks and to focus on uncertainties. But the more we know, the more we also realize what we do not know as yet.

Uncertainty is an inherent component of the process of research. It resides in the multiple ways of searching for and generating new knowledge. Discovery is open-ended and fundamental research cannot predict what it will find or when.

Research is the basis of a powerful and systematic process that seeks to transform uncertainties into certainties, only to be confronted with new uncertainties again. Scientific certainties are carefully couched in the precise terms of the conditions under which they hold. Moreover, they are always preliminary. They can and most likely will be replaced by new knowledge, sidestepped by new certainties. Together with curiosity, the lure of uncertainty and of discovering what was not known before is the driving force in this domain of creative human endeavor. If the belief in progress of science and technology and the possibilities for intervention it opens has never waned in the scientific community, this is not always the case in society. The challenge for science to share the sense of intimate involvement in embracing uncertainty with society of which it is a part, so goes my argument, increases together with the capability of science of confronting uncertainty.

At present, the fissure of how to deal, let alone cope, with uncertainty marks the relationship between science and society. While "society," this volatile and hard to grasp assemblage of alternating publics, organized groups in civil society, engaged and dissatisfied citizens and the media, may share some knowledge with experts in making technical judgements, significant differences remain. The line between the prerogative of experts in making technical judgements, including those pertaining to the respective degree of certainty, and the prerogative of non-experts to assess the consequences of those judgements, is a fine one to tread (Collins 2014). Between these positions lies the vast range of unintended consequences of human action. It takes us into the realm of complexity in which properties and the behavior of a system are not determined by its parts, but by their interaction. Seeking to reduce the hidden uncertainties that arise through these interactions will be one of the major tasks ahead. It mutually implicates science and society, as neither can succeed without the other.

Uncertainty is not only embodied and enacted in notions of the future or in the domain of knowledge production. It is a well-known feature of organizational life. Every institution and social organization encounters and needs to cope with uncertainty all the time. In different ways, they are confronted with changes in their environment. They crave for success and efficiency, however defined, and know that they must continue to learn from mistakes and from the ambiguity of their experience. This necessitates adaptation, anticipation, preparedness and even innovation. Depending on their goals and specific organizational forms, available resources, leadership and power relations, institutions seek to reduce uncertainty. They also exploit it for their own purposes and/or accommodate it by a muddling-through approach. These elements overlap and vary.

Uncertainty for institutions and how to deal with it comes in different guises. Due to the enduring crisis they unleashed, financial markets have been catapulted into the center of public scrutiny, outrage and timid attempts at more and tighter regulation. They have been criticized for having been fooled by randomness as they failed to recognize the non-normality of events under their remit. More concretely, they are criticized for having committed the policy error of not distinguishing risk from uncertainty. Thus, they largely missed the non-normality that may result in the escalation of uncertainties, leading to potentially catastrophic phase shifts (Haldane 2012). Uncertainties in this peculiar institutional environment offer fascinating glimpses on how simulation models and insights into the dynamics of complex adaptive systems can uncover yet another dimension of the unintended consequences of human action.

One uncertainty that many institutions have to deal with is the uncertainty of future success. This is often intimately tied to people, the human resources of any organization. Initiated by new public management practices, a noticeable trend has been the widespread introduction of quantitative indicators and various kinds of impact assessments. Obviously, this influences the recruitment and selection of people, but also the (re)distribution of responsibility across different levels of hierarchies. As a consequence, uncertainty is shifted elsewhere.

Humanity has made impressive strides in moving from acceptance of what was perceived as fate and the inevitability of destiny towards attempts to shape the human condition in its material, cultural, political, social and organizational dimensions. The various historical trajectories display no lack of arrogance and hubris, of chaotic failures, of overconfidence and the ensuing catastrophes. Yet, once the future became conceived as an open horizon, whatever the weight and burden of path-dependence in history, it provided the possibility of escaping the inevitability of a strict determinism. The future became seen as truly uncertain. From then onwards, to accept reality as it is made it possible to assert that it could have happened otherwise. Which brings me to the second main theme of this book: the cunning of uncertainty.

The argument presented here is that, in the various manifestations and enactments of uncertainty, the logic of its cunning is at work in the ways we encounter and engage with it. Uncertainty is never completely static but is a process that does not cease to evolve. It encompasses extremely long timescales and, on the level of human experience, also very short ones. Decisions over life and death may be taken in the blink of the eye, while human interactions with the natural environment may reveal their impact only in geological timescales. The cunning of uncertainty may manifest itself in the choice of the right moment. Timing is also cunning.

Uncertainty is often embedded in situations of ambiguity where it is difficult to disentangle what is known in principle but not in the practice of what is not (yet) known, even if practical action must be taken. The distinction between risk and uncertainty also continues to shift over time. Advances of science and technology in conjunction with novel forms of organization and social innovation transform former uncertainties into risks. Simultaneously, systemic risks that were invisible until now come into sight.

The cunning of uncertainty is a subversive force of reasoning and action. It bears resemblance to the cunning of reason, which for the ancient Greeks was embodied in metis. It is seen in action alongside episteme and plays an important role in Homer and in Greek drama. According to Detienne and Vernant, it:

> ...[I]mplies a complex but very coherent body of mental attitudes and intellectual behaviour which combines flair, wisdom,

> forethought, subtlety of mind, deception, resourcefulness, vigilance, opportunism, various skills and experience acquired over the years. It is applied to situations which are transient, shifting, disconcerting and ambiguous, situations which do not lend themselves to precise measurements, exact calculation or vigorous logic (Detienne and Vernant 1978).
>
> The English word cunning has the same etymological root as the German kennen and können. It is knowledge that combines knowing and crafting. Einstein and Bacon admitted cunning reason as an integral part of their epistemology and in their interactionist realism (Elkana 1981).

The cunning of uncertainty can be captured by thick descriptions in its many empirical instantiations. It appears at unexpected moments. Its logic shuns the direct line. It indulges in taking the oblique route and occasionally unexpected shortcuts. In science, serendipity—the unexpected finding of something one was not looking for yet whose significance one recognizes—is a highly welcome and recognized form of cunning when wrestling with uncertainty. In the context of contemporary societies, the cunning of uncertainty may act as a wholesome counterforce to the false certainties induced by hubris and over-reliance on the assumptions that undergird what people think they know. The cunning of uncertainty excels in uncovering the unintended consequences of human purposeful action. It helps to tease out what one is unable to see otherwise when fixing one's gaze on specific goals, even when acting with the best intentions. Experience shows that what has been actually achieved usually differs substantially from what was intended. The cunning of uncertainty courts surprise and invites the unexpected. It upturns routine and is a guide to seeing the potential which has not yet had a real opportunity to unfold and flourish. It excels in luring us to make promises and to believe in promises made by others.

The more the cunning of uncertainty is acknowledged and recognized, so my argument goes, the less the need to feel threatened by uncertainty. The cloak of its presumed inevitability is then revealed to be full of holes. Probabilities take the place of determinism, only to be superseded by the probabilities of probability distributions. The cunning of uncertainty opens new spaces and facilitates alternative options to emerge. Ambiguities permit boundary crossings where closure between knowledge domains or areas of strictly defined expertise reigned before. Ambiguities do not mean that everything becomes fuzzy and porous or that anything goes. It means acknowledging that social life is full of contradictions and that social beings have the ability to navigate between them. Once they have the necessary resources, they also negotiate with each other viable options for living together. The last part of my argument rests upon personal experience.

Having spent my professional life studying science as a system and scientists as the main protagonists in a social context which at times appears contradictory and bewildering to them, I remain struck by the different approaches towards uncertainty. In science, a culture of embracing uncertainty reigns, even if many researchers are busy in their daily work routine to solidify knowledge claims and to utilize the certainties so far achieved in specific contexts of application.

In the policy context, the confidence of dealing with uncertainty is put to an often harsh test. Not only are politicians hard to convince to invest in fundamental research whose outcome is highly uncertain, as it cannot be predicted. For them, funding short-term projects with economic impact remains the more attractive item on the political agenda. Short-term small gains trump long-term but uncertain high gain opportunities. Policy advice remains a contested and murky endeavor in the political arena. It is not easy to detect and to fill the rightful place of science. Even if assessments of risks and uncertainty were to converge, consensus on the action to be taken as a consequence most likely will not.

Such fundamental differences in approach were brought home to me during the years spent in helping to establish and operate the European Research Council (ERC), set up in 2007. The European Commission took a radical step in entrusting the setting of the strategy for this new funding institution to a group of independent scientists. Autonomous space was thus created for the best ideas, bottom-up, without setting thematic priorities and committing to scientific excellence only. If science does thrive on the cusp of uncertainty, here was the cusp. It stretched right across all scientific disciplines in a radical openness for the cutting edge of science. It was wholeheartedly committed to promoting outstanding talent, especially among the younger generation. As my colleagues and I soon were to discover, this culture of trust, which felt at ease with uncertainty, encountered an administrative culture of control with a very low tolerance level for uncertainty. Over time, against many odds and with some difficulties, both sides managed to set up a research funding organization which performs at world-class level. With some cunning, uncertainty that is inherent in fundamental research succeeded in carving out a niche in which it can flourish.

Of course, I realize that the preconditions and framings for welcoming uncertainty in science are carefully specified and circumscribed. Every experiment is a process deeply marked by uncertainty. On the one hand, the possible is invited to occur. Somehow on the other hand, what is possible must already have been decided before. Outside the lab, the conditions become even more stringent. Tolerance of uncertainty meets its limits when the stress of materials in buildings or bridges has to be calculated, when air traffic and safety regulations are simulated or the admission of new drugs on the market undergo a series of strictly controlled clinical trials. Safety concerns must override the playful engagement with uncertainty. But in the real world, things can become messy very quickly. Distinctions between acceptable risks and those deemed unacceptable are not easy to make. Legal rules and regulations can lead to a considerable restraint on action and exploration. This is further exacerbated once people begin to worry that they might be sued, leading to institutional inertia and individual anticipatory compliance.

One argument against a more proactive and positive engagement with uncertainty in society is that this is pure luxury, a concern of the elite. As long as people live under conditions of basic insecurity or are thrown back again into it through rising inequalities and an extremely precarious labor market, the accumulation of their economic and social disadvantages sets different priorities for them. While there is some truth to the argument, as security is a fundamental necessity and insecurity must not be confused with uncertainty, research shows that even people living under very precarious economic and social conditions display a considerable amount of social resilience. This is the capacity of groups or societies to bind together in order to sustain and advance their well-being in the face of challenges, including those that arise from the presently dominant economic regime. Social resilience is a dynamic process. Well-being is conditioned by the balance between the life challenges people face and their capabilities for coping with them. They depend on access not only to economic resources, but also to cultural and social resources (Hall and Lamont 2013). Learning to cope with uncertainty is one of the most precious cultural resources. This is one more reason why it must be shared and access to it facilitated.

If coping with uncertainty is an important cultural resource, it will be in even greater demand in the future. According to Organisation for Economic Co-operation and Development statistics, job profiles are changing and so is the demand for skills. With routine jobs in decline, the demand for non-routine skills goes up. These include the capacity to deal with unexpected situations and uncertainty. The question arises: how good are we in educating young people for uncertainty, while continuing to train them for certainty? There is a widespread feeling of unease today, triggered by the financial and economic crisis, but also by growing signs of geopolitical instability. This feeling is reinforced by a widespread outlook on the future as fragile and precarious, with climate change harboring yet more ominous possibilities. The feeling of crisis is always concentrated in the present. In its own momentousness, it signals the non-normality of what is experienced now. Yet, once we are ready to move beyond the tautology of what is to be considered normal, a larger picture emerges. It is populated by black swans and extreme events, by power-laws and non-linear dynamics that arise from interactions we are otherwise unable to detect. It is a picture of deep uncertainty. Yet, at the samc time, based on models of biological evolution and of social evolution and resilience, new approaches to cope with risk under conditions of uncertainty emerge.

If we are ready to see the future as a cultural fact, as Arjun Appadurai suggests, the future is something which can be made but also something which is still to be made. As a cultural fact, it is a collective effort, to be built on some kind of shared vision. But it also takes all the cultural resources we can muster. Science and technology have put an amazing amount of such resources at our disposal. They include the modelling of complex adaptive systems and the insights that are to be gained by making visible what otherwise remains invisible: the unintended consequences of human action. Yet whatever resources science and technology have to offer, they are not sufficient if they do not find their way back into the social context.

For the context is and remains society. It is a messy mixture of institutional inertia and over-cautiousness, of vested interests and power structures, of path-dependence including many errors which have been neither acknowledged nor corrected. Yet, in the delicate and tension-ridden relationship between science and society, this is all we have. Democracy is under pressure to re-invent itself and science will soon realize that it is not sufficient to only communicate science. The challenge is to look, think and move beyond the current imperatives of accountability and innovation.

Meanwhile, the cunning of uncertainty is willing to direct those who trust its subversive lead to some of the many situated loci in which uncertainty resides. It is willing to offer cunning access to some of the latest knowledge tools, things to think with and mix with practice. It widens the scope for prediction, while showing the limitations of what can be predicted. As all other knowledge, this is provisional and evolves according to its own dynamic and in an unpredictable way. It comes with a promise: it could be otherwise.

References

Collins, Harry M. *Are We All Scientific Experts Now?* Cambridge: Cambridge University Press, 2014.

Detienne, Marcel and Jean-Pierre Vernant. *Cunning Intelligence in Greek Culture and Society.* Sussex: Harvester Press, Hassocks, 1978.

Elkana, Yehuda. "A Programmatic Attempt at an Anthropology of Knowledge." In *Sciences and Cultures. Sociology of the Sciences a Yearbook, vol. 5*, edited by Everett Mendelsohn and Yehuda Elkana, 1–76. Dordrecht: Reidel, 1981.

Haldane, Andrew G. "Tails of the Unexpected." Speech, "The Credit Crisis Five Years On: Unpacking the Crisis," University of Edinburgh Business School, June 8, 2012. Bank of England. https://www.bankofengland.co.uk/speech/2012/tails-of-the-unexpected.

Hall, Peter and Michèle Lamont, ed. *Social Resilience in the Neoliberal Era.* Cambridge: Cambridge University Press, 2013.

II.

Introduction to *Cultures of Technology and the Quest for Innovation*[*]

This volume edited by me deals with technology, innovation, and culture. It focuses on why culture matters for technology and the significance attributed to the ubiquitous and unrelenting quest for innovation since the onset of modernity. Innovation comes with promises of human betterment and the will to control. It is a bet on the future, which is seen as offering unbounded opportunities and creates a highly competitive economic environment. It introduces new kinds of risks and the anxieties that come with it. Retracing historical precedents, I conclude that the quest for innovation fills a conceptual void that can partly be explained by the altered relationship between State and Market. Technological innovation acts as a proxy for construction of a shared sense of the future. It mobilizes resources that are indispensable and stimulates public discourse intended as a prelude for social acceptance.

---

[*] Originally published in Helga Nowotny, ed., "Introduction: The Quest for Innovation and Cultures of Technology," in *Cultures of Technology and the Quest for Innovation* (New York: Berghahn Books, 2006), 1–23. This is an abridged version of the original work.

Looking at technological innovation through a cultural lens is demanding but widens the perspective. Much can be gained by conceiving of technology not just as an ensemble of artifacts or complex socio-technical systems. Culture is about social relations with meanings attached to what people do, believe, and how they relate to each other and to the environment through the technologies they produce and use. Technological culture thus renders the technical artifacts visible as an integral part of the "web of significance" that humans continue to spin for themselves. In many practical ways, technology mediates and transforms, acts and is acted upon. It can short-circuit decision-making and the arduous process of finding consensus.

Looking back from today's point of view on what I wrote twenty years ago, it seems more urgent than before to take up these strands of thought from where I ended. The digital world we inhabit challenges us to interweave a highly sophisticated and powerful digital technology with meaning. We still need to find a sense of purpose and direction that integrates what digital technologies have to offer with a shared vision of the future. We lack a culture of AI. The digital Web and everything connected to it is yet to be transformed into a "web of significance," created through the co-evolution of human agency with the potential embodied by technology.

❐❑❐

It is impossible to imagine the future without referring to the concept of innovation. Like an almost invisible tether suspended from a spaceship, the quest for innovation is taking measurements in an unknown environment. Its bearings are confined to the tiny base in which it has been set up, while the surrounding space is vast, cold, and indifferent. And yet, this quest continues its exploration, fueled by human ingenuity and driven by insatiable curiosity. Built as a result of today's scientific and technological knowledge and the range of skills available at present, it extends forward in time and is guided by what human imagination and determination have to offer: vague promises of improvement, the desire to understand, and hence the will to control. Never before in our history has there been such a view of the future that offers unbounded opportunities. While science and technology make innovations possible at an unprecedented rate, the social order—and especially the economic organization of today's societies—have created a culture of competition and economic growth that continues to extend the horizon toward the unknown future. With the onset of modernity, contingencies were embraced. Now we are being asked to embrace the inherent uncertainty residing in the endless process of innovation.

The Future of the Past

While today the future appears to be highly uncertain and fragile, exacerbated by the relentlessly ongoing process of globalization and, more recently, of the fear of the further spread of global terrorism, the view of the future was very different only thirty years ago. Looking backward may therefore throw light on what has changed. Perhaps no other book is such a compelling witness as *The Limits to Growth* (Meadows et al. 1972) published under the auspices of the Club of Rome. This ambitious research project triggered an unprecedented worldwide response since it was the first computer-based world model with normative assumptions, which had emerged from the young field of dynamic systems modeling. Some interpreted it as a courageous attempt to confront in a holistic way all of the pressing problems of the world, while others, especially other academics, were more skeptical in their assessments. But even they had to concede that the public response to the study was impressive. One review headline read, "The Computer that Printed Out W*O*L*F." The "wolf" that had allegedly been sighted, however, was more than a mere figment of the imagination on the part of a world in crisis. The book represented a thinly disguised attack on one of the era's hitherto unquestioned ideological dogmas. It contained the sharpest possible warning of the environmental and demographic consequences of a commitment to the project of continued, undifferentiated, and unimpeded economic growth. According to the authors and to their sponsor, this was the real cause underlying the most urgent problems facing humanity. The various crisis scenarios that the model produced demanded action, as well as a reversal of the dominant thinking, if humanity and its relentless exploitation of the environment were to be pulled back from the abyss at the last possible moment.

It is quite intriguing to look back at the projections of a future that by now has become the past (Nowotny 2002). It may seem paradoxical to claim that one of the more lasting legacies of *The Limits to Growth* has been an altered sense of the future and of the ways of coping with its inherent fragility. While the world models of J. W. Forrester and D. L. Meadows were being devised, the future was considered predictable to a degree. The belief in its predictability underpinned the strong media response elicited by the computer-generated consequences. Based upon this belief it was possible to link the results that had been obtained through mathematical probabilities to the starkly normative claims that accompanied them, namely, that it was mandatory to change individual and collective behavior, and the economy and politics in a way that would prevent the collapse otherwise predicted.

Today's sense of the future could not be more different. It is spoken about in the conditional, and should be used exclusively as a plural despite the linguistic oddity. Uncertainties and contingencies abound. Various kinds of risks, of different proportions and subject to varying perceptions, have become an integral part of our lives, replacing the fear of the one big catastrophe that loomed large in the 1970s: the collapse of the environment. Even the latest spread of fears—fear of an enemy who is believed to be capable of the most wanton acts of destruction—fits into this overall picture, despite the difference in scale and content. The future has therefore moved closer to the present. Concomitantly, the tools to imagine the future in a more systematic way have also evolved. Models are recognized as being provisional; they capture a fluctuating present in a conjectural mode that projects certain assumptions and their dynamics. The process of thinking through, and reflecting upon, one's built-in assumptions has become far more important than the actual findings. Results of the process of modeling are clearly seen to possess a highly preliminary and precarious status. In using the various tools of forecasting or of backcasting, of future scanning or devising road maps, of creating visions or of celebrating the creative forces of chaos, flexibility and creativity have become the hallmarks of this process. In its exuberant rhetoric, the process mirrors the predominant mechanism, which is widely believed to incarnate the promise of optimal adaptation to the uncertainties of the future: the market.

The links between the present and the unknown future have always been a source of fascination, and each culture, each historical epoch, has structured them in diverse ways. The urge to divine what was to come lay at the roots of the ancient Chinese arts of numbers and mathematics. Christian theology pictured a future based upon the belief in salvation. And, for probably most of our history, fate reigned supreme in many societies. With modernity came the belief that the future could be planned, at least to a certain degree. The advances made in such fields of knowledge as mathematical probability theory enabled new social institutions to gain an economically viable footing, and to be able to cope with the unknowns of the future. The promises of modernity were also premised upon a new confidence in the achievements of an increasingly self-governing society. Today, our public belief is that innovation enable us to negotiate the future, after having had to accept that there are limits to planning. Innovation embraces the uncertainties inherent in the future—and attempts to seize whatever opportunities they have to offer. The meaning of the concept of innovation has been changed. While the configuration of known elements is still at its core, it also transcends what is known in a radical, evolutionary sense.

Why has the quest for innovation become so omnipresent at the beginning of the 21st century? When and how did the collective obsession with innovation arise—not only on the rhetoric of politics, which always carries promises of a better future, but also among industrialists who seek to adapt to the new economy of increasing returns (Arthur 1996) and to play the high-tech game. Even the quest for discoveries, whose significance as an indispensable epistemic base is sometimes realized only much later, is now moving closer to possible technological applications. Most scientists are aware of the fact that they are also expected to seek possible ways of "translating" their basic findings and discoveries that will be useful to society in one way or another. While curiosity has not disappeared, it too now takes part in the dominant motivation for engaging in research.

The current emphasis on innovation does not mean that this is a new phenomenon, nor that innovation was not seen as highly desirable and crucial for economic growth before. But—to mention one example—innovation processes are understood as endogenous phenomena in orthodox neoclassical economic theory. To this day, J. A. Schumpeter's proposals for an economic theory of innovation remain outside mainstream economic thought. Economists who took them as a starting point for modeling techniques, or who wanted to consider processes of innovation empirically, depart critically from neoclassical theory. Empirically speaking, processes of innovation are the result of specific activities aimed at changing the production process or at introducing new products; their result cannot be forecasted in detail. The whole problematic lies in the unpredictability of the success of attempts at innovation. Investments in innovation cannot be derived rationally due to the strategic uncertainty with respect to the action of other actors and to the uncertainty of the utility of the innovation. As Schumpeter (1934) argued a long time ago in *The Theory of Economic Development*, entrepreneurs are indeed interested in profit, but innovation cannot be understood as motivated by goal oriented utility maximizing alone (Beckert 2002).

One theme I want to propose here is that the quest for innovation fills a conceptual void in our collective imagining of the future. This is an important void, insofar as it holds the key to a future that otherwise escapes us. Our thinking about the future is itself historically constrained. It has moved precariously between some degree of stability and a principled openness to the unforeseen. It has become subject to an evolutionary perspective, which brings with it a notion of radical openness. Our projections of the future have begun to oscillate between the emerging order on the one hand, and the edge of chaos on the other hand. Against the background of our growing knowledge about the dynamics of complex systems, thinking about the future has become less mechanistic and naive. It has perhaps even become reflexive in the sense that thinking about the future is no longer primarily based upon "what is likely to happen." Questions have shifted toward knowledge of the actors imagining different kinds of futures. In one domain in particular, financial markets, this kind of reasoning, and the mathematical tools that accompany it, have reached an impressive level of sophistication (Bernstein 1996).

The conceptual void arises for many different reasons. One of the reasons, however, emerges from the changing nature of the relationship between the state and the market. Because innovation is both a socioeconomic and a technological process, the support for innovation and entrepreneurship is increasingly seen as being also a pro-active responsibility of governments. In their classic book, *How the West Grew Rich*, Nathan Rosenberg and L. E. Birdzell Jr. wrote in 1985: "In all well-ordered societies, political authority is dedicated to stability, security, and the status quo. It is thus singularly ill-qualified to direct, or channel activity intended to produce instability, insecurity, and change" (Rosenberg and Birdzell 1985). Today, all highly industrialized nation-states have developed a set of policy tools to foster technological innovation and investment in research. While technological innovation in a more narrow or technical sense still occurs and can therefore be defined as "the successful implementation (in commerce or management) of a technical new idea to the institution creating it" (Branscomb 2001) or as "the process by which firms master and get into practice product designs and manufacturing processes that are new to them..." (Nelson 1993), it is now recognized that what is required is an innovative society.

Political agendas aimed at promoting technological innovation, including "foresight" exercises of various kinds, thus serve as proxies for constructing a shared vision of the future. This process is in turn indicative of the necessity to cope in both an active and an interactive fashion with the fragmentary and undecided nature of what we regard to be the future. There is a growing realization that innovation processes do not automatically follow from the results of research, whatever their potential may be. The "linear model," which foresees that basic research will somehow find its way to being transferred or translated into applied research, which will in turn later appear on the market in the form of commercially viable products or processes, appears as an idealized version of what happened in a given historical period, namely, after World War II (Gibbons et al. 1994). Nor can today's innovation processes be left to entrepreneurs alone, however strong their "restlessness" (in a Schumpeterian sense) may be. The omnipresent quest for innovation, caught up as it has been in a globalized world, is a hybrid of many elements. It includes the availability of venture capital and the creativity of determined individuals, as much as the flexibility of institutions and regulatory processes. An ever-expanding knowledge base and the appropriate research system must be in tune as well with the wider expectations of society, whose ultimate acceptance will be decisive. Innovation stands for social change, which is embraced by some and feared by others. And, as with modernity's previous march forward, there will be winners and losers. Innovation also faces barriers that are much more difficult to detect, because they inhere in the nature of institutions and of large sociotechnical systems. Nor does innovation necessarily always offer the best technological solutions. Technology can become locked-in, as can innovations. All this is part of a public discourse intent on moving forward toward an uncertain future.

An Historical Precedent

It is tempting to compare the recent emergence of innovation as a major concept of our time to an historical precedent. In a curious twist, concepts that are taken for granted are often projected backward into the past as though they had always existed. Leo Marx has shown that this occurred in the 19th century with the then-novel concept of technology (Marx 1997). The belated emergence of the word technology, used to name what allegedly was driving history during the mid-19th century in the United States, is a reminder of how an old word can be invested with new meaning, and thus often serves as a marker for far-reaching developments and for ongoing changes in a society and in its culture.

During the 1840s in the United States two kinds of large-scale changes had become apparent, one ideological, involving the prevailing ideas about the mechanical arts, the other substantive, affecting the organizational and material matrix of the mechanical arts. Webster's audience no longer thought of the railroad as merely a means to achieving social and political progress. For the new entrepreneurial elite, the mechanical arts were highly visible, and this change was ripe for the emergence of a new word: technology. The blurring of the distinction between mechanical means and political or normative ends, however, did meet with strong criticism.

The second substantive change occurred in the material and organizational character of the mechanical arts. The change was embodied in machines, but in the second half of the 19th century the machine was replaced by a new kind of sociotechnological system. The railroad was among the earliest and most visible, large-scale technological systems of its time. A novel feature of such a system is that the crucial mechanical component, the physical artifact itself, constitutes only a small part of the whole. Concomitantly, the organizational features that were required to render it operational have expanded tremendously, from ancillary equipment and large corporate business organizations with unprecedented capital investment, all the way to the new sets of skills required from the workforce. While the merger of science and the practical arts and industry was already underway, it was not until the end of the century with the growth of the electrical and chemical industries that the transformative power of the new entity—now called technology—became fully visible. And, as so often before, a pioneer had already been using the word far ahead of his time. It was a Boston botanist and physician, Jacob Bigelow, who as early as 1826, "adopted the general name of Technology, a word sufficiently expressive" to denote "the practical applications of science, which may be considered useful, by promoting the benefit of society, together with the emolument of those who pursue them." The greatest success in dissemination came when the term technology was used in naming a new institution of higher learning, the Massachusetts Institute of Technology, now better known as MIT, in 1862 (Webster 1903).

Innovation Fills the Void

The quest for innovation fills another conceptual void, and it has taken on a new meaning as a response to the profound changes going on in our time. On the ideological level, the belief in progress, at least as naively understood in the 19th and in most of the 20th centuries, has been dealt major blows, from which it has been unable to recover. The dream of the Enlightenment thinkers—that science and technology would be a means to the ends of social improvement and political emancipation—was short-lived. As Bertrand Russell and others have pointed out, science does not free humanity from its most violent passions; on the contrary, it may even fuel them. Technology has revealed itself to be an assistant to humanity in acts of the most horrible destruction and brutality. Scientific and technical progress has not prevented society from falling back into a state of incredibly cruel destruction and barbarity, of which the 20th century had more than its share. Whatever gains in productivity have been achieved as a result of science and technology, we must conclude that they have not brought with them a concomitant improvement in moral standards and behavior.

Closer to the present, the tangible burdens of unrelenting technological advances have become more visible and, even as we strive to eliminate or contain them as much as possible, the unintended consequences of increasing intervention in the natural and social environment are here to stay. The shock wave created in the late 1960s and early 1970s by books such as Rachel Carson's *Silent Spring* (1962) or Meadow's *Limits to Growth* (1972) brought awareness of an ongoing environmental degradation and the onset of the much-vaunted risk society. While some of the environmental problems have been alleviated, others have merely been transformed into increasing global inequalities. The demand for sustainability in interacting with the natural environment has, in conjunction with technological improvements, led to some beneficial results, although the final verdict as to where we now stand remains inconclusive. What has changed, however, is the perception of risks. The environmental agenda today is dominated by the major theme of global climate change and its anthropogenic origins. The threat it poses is quite serious since it represents the unpredictable: for extreme changes in weather and for extreme oscillations of climate. It spells unknown variability, both locally and regionally, and is imbued with a sense of human impotence. Faced with these unknowns, the only valid prediction seems to be "to expect the unexpected"—which hardly offers a solid basis for future interventions.

On the substantive-organizational side, the impact of science and technology on our lives is even greater. The large sociotechnical systems that were the pride of modernity are still with us, although they have acquired a bewildering complexity. Due to the unabated and worldwide spread of the power of computers, these systems have been partly decentralized and continue to promote processes of globalization. Jobs are outsourced to less developed countries where the percentage of a technologically savvy, highly skilled labor force is on the increase. The world of the factory, characterized by planning, control, and hierarchy and in which bulk material was processed and production optimization strived for, has yielded in part to a high-tech world based on the processing of information. This new world is characterized by flattened hierarchies, by technologies depending upon other products and other technologies, by missions, by teams, and by cunning. Operations once handled by people are now handled by software. Adaptation to an ever-changing environment reigns supreme (Arthur 1996).

With the shift from the state to market forces, national boundaries have not only become easier to cross, but this may now function as incentive or obstacle for the creation of jobs and for increasing market shares. While the modern, pre-World War II managerial and engineering approach associates management with large manufacturing firms, the post-World War II approach associates management with projects that introduce new technological systems, such as computer networks and urban highways. They are no longer committed to maintaining a system for the mass production of standardized items. They tolerate and even embrace heterogeneity. They expect discontinuous change and brace themselves to manage innovation on a day-to-day basis in a world of complexity. Thomas P. Hughes has juxtaposed the characteristics of what he calls modern and postmodern project and technology management, and the comparison offers a striking contract. Modern and postmodern project management excels in hierarchical and centralized control mechanisms and structures, tightly coupled system, and homogeneity. Technology management relies on an often horizontal networked control, which is loosely coupled and thrives on heterogeneity. Heterogeneous agents control this technological culture, but this can no longer be exerted in a centralized mode. The best that such agents can do is to monitor the complex development of technology. There agents include industrial corporation, research laboratories, academia, the military, local and national governments, and "the will of the people" (Hughes 1998).

This shift of regime is marked by a profound transformation of both the technology itself and the context in which it works. It is a shift in scale that marks a shift in time and space, that makes possible new forms of time management, and that opens up new sites as a result of its functioning: sites that it then uses in the course of its functioning. It can perhaps best be summarized as a shift from exotechnologies to endotechnologies. Technology as it has existed since time immemorial, which enabled our ancestors to survive, has been commensurate in scale with that of the human habitat. Even when the sheer reach of the human habitat was vastly extended—with the use of such modes of transportation as ships, cars, and airplanes—the goal of technology was to serve the function that archaeologists and anthropologists insist upon: to enlarge the biologically restricted human reach in its immediate and geographically extended environment. Such exotechnologies have enabled us to cross larger distances in less time; they have also allowed for the mass production of artifacts as well as for the construction of vast infrastructures for a variety of purposes, from growing, transporting, and conserving food and other products to living in growing comfort in a variety of climates.

The new regime of endotechnologies—biotechnologies and nanotechnologies, together with information technologies and other enabling, symbolic technologies—is extending the scale of the human-built world down to that of infinitesimal living organisms and within matter itself. It transforms the management of time in the sense that those genetic mechanisms which, for instance, induces the growth of plants, can now be reversed, while natural aging processes can be speeded up or delayed. Electricity once allowed us to extend our use of daytime and indeed to turn night into day. This same effect is now made possible by our intervention into the circadian rhythm and by our switching genes on and off. Endotechnologies transform space by opening up living organisms and by turning them into the site of intervention. Living organisms and the creation of life, and the dynamics of growth and decline at different levels in the hierarchy of living matter, all these make possible novel forms of time management.

In 1959, at the annual meeting of the American Physical Society, Richard Feynman gave his classic lecture, "There's Plenty of Room at the Bottom," about the prospect of manipulating objects on a small scale; he understood with astonishing foresight that the molecular structure of matter would become another prime site for new endotechnological procedures. Individual atoms can now be assembled and reassembled at will. New properties can be designed to build new materials. The "creative force of the created object" at work here comes from the growth of computers, which has enabled us to generate, process, and retrieve data on an unprecedented scale. This creative force is inherent in technical devices like the polymerase chain reaction (PCR) allowing the mass sequencing of genes. In the words of Paul Rabinow, "PCR is more than the possibilities of its applications.

It possesses the quality to enable new events" (Rabinow 1996). Many other methods and devices, and instruments and instrumentations exist, which all work together to make possible new events on unprecedentedly small scales. The growing inter- or transdisciplinary convergence of mathematics, biology, physics, chemistry, information technology, and statistics, brings approaches and methods to bear on commonly defined problems. Biology is taking great strides toward becoming integrative, starting with the molecular level.

These developments, while being greeted enthusiastically by the scientific community, also create a lot of unease in the wider society. They raise such questions as what it means to be human, who defines what is "natural," and what is considered "cultural." By extending the impact of technologies not only toward the environment, but by directing them inside living organisms, science has given rise to anxiety equivalent to the wonder it has inspired. With every new scientific and technological advance, the number of options increases, yet it is impossible to foresee many of the consequences. Uncertainties abound and have become inherent to the process of producing new knowledge. The view of the future, as we have seen, has become fraught with uncertainties. There is, however, no turning back. As the number of potential future options grows, the number of escape routes diminishes. Fundamentalism, whether or not religious, remains one of the few alternatives, but its appeal is limited. The utopia of modernity has become exhausted, since the promises of modernity have been partly fulfilled. But when desire and reality do not match, discontent remains. We have to move forward toward a highly uncertain future—but how?

Contrary to Bruno Latour's proposition that "we have never been modern" (Latour 1993), we are all modern today. And contrary to other postmodern beliefs, we are condemned to remain modern for some time to come. But modernity is no longer a program that will deliver—it has already delivered the building blocks, the institutions and structures we use. It fails to respond to expectations. It is no substitute for the belief in progress that served to underpin modernity until it collapsed under the weight of the hype it carried. With the future open, the challenge lies in the belief that worthwhile novelty will emerge with power sufficient to generate further worthwhile novelties, which will in turn lead to further economic growth and well-being is inevitable. This process should be sufficiently open to incorporate human values, like forging sustainable links to the natural environment or furthering education as a means of social inclusion. There is other strongly held values that have emerged, such as the value attached to security. But how to translate such values and their internal contradictions into a concept that will fill the void? The only other concept (or Denkfigur in the sense of Ludwik Fleck) that would offer a credible alternative is evolution. Taking the concept out of its original biologic domain of meaning and transferring it metaphorically to the social and cultural domain, however, has proven to be extremely tricky (Campbell 1975, 1969). Moreover, evolution, after having stripped the world of divine intervention, also leaves no room for human agency.

Innovation is a concept that crosses domains easily. It can take up residence in the cultural domain and in social organizations, indeed in every field in which human creativity flourishes. Innovation signals the positive direction where the unknown is to be found, and it is therefore reassuring. In contrast to the concept of technology, innovation cannot be transformed into an object since it is a process, amenable to action and interaction, even if it carries its own load of uncertainty. But there is the chance that opportunities will outweigh whatever negative consequences the future has in store.

The meaning of innovation is affected by these processes as well. It is no longer, as Schumpeter in his classical analysis at the beginning of the 20th century saw as "merely" a recombination of known factors that enables the entrepreneurial individual to gain a decisive advantage over the competition. Important and widespread as this recombinatorial form of innovation remains, a more extended notion of innovation, based on the potential of "radical" novelty and therefore embracing the uncertainty inherent, has emerged. As early as the 1970s, the economist G. L. S. Shackle spoke about "essential novelty" as idiosyncratic of an evolutionary approach in techno-social innovations that includes openness toward an unknown future (Shackle 1969). Seen from an economic perspective, innovation presupposes contingencies and choices that transcend a recombination of what already exists.

Innovation fills the void that arises out of the genuine uncertainty inherent in the process of innovation itself. Paradoxically, it is due to this circularity—or modern reflexivity—of innovation that it has the ability to fill this void. It is not an unmoved mover behind the impersonal forces of a technocratic society, as it might have been the case not too long ago. Technocracy itself, as a recognizable structure, is being undone by innovation only to be reconfigured as a widely dispersed, interlocking form of governance in which not only corporate actors and governments, but also civil society, interact in a conflict-ridden struggle for the newly emerging global order. Innovation is the only credible response currently available for coping with the uncertainty it has helped to generate. It is credible in the sense that it does not preclude plurality, diversity, or variation. On the contrary, it invites and thrives on them. Innovation—although its direction is heavily biased toward scientific-technological advances—does not preclude manifestation in other domains: social innovations, for instance, which might bring about other forms of governance, with the task of integrating the current skepticism and prevailing unease with regard to certain technological innovations. It does not preclude the possibility of new forms of cultural innovation, with the arts confronting the way in which the disturbances emanate from the latest run of feasible scientific-technical breakthroughs (Nowotny 2003). Innovation is called for everywhere—and not precluded anywhere. This is why it is credible.

Innovation invites human agency and depends upon it—where would it come from otherwise? Technological developments merely provide opportunities, and it is up to us, individually as well as collectively, to act upon them. It does not predetermine any specific end result. The only determinant it resolutely insists upon is the option of change. It plays with the ambiguities entailed by embracing change when the goal is not fixed, but reassures us that human action may shape what is to come. Dealing with risks? No problem, since you may adopt the precautionary principle. You may also choose not to espouse the apocalyptic warnings contained in the "risk-society" and instead opt for a "modern" risk culture as it is embodied by the global financial markets. These are institutions that depend not only upon infrastructures and material resources, but have also adopted a specific risk culture, "an entrenched set of practices of market configuration, technological development, social group construction, and notions of authority, expertise, and creativity which combines modernity's ambition to know with the market's ambition to commodify" (Green 2000). The argument of choice, so deeply entrenched both in neoliberal economics and liberal democracies, has benefited the empowerment of consumers, without always assuring that the preconditions for exerting choice are being met.

In brief, the concept of innovation is closer than other concepts, like the "knowledge society" (which invokes counter concepts, e.g., ignorance and the right not to know), to the continuity of an iterative modernity, punctuated as may be the case by relapses into recurrent crises and into periods of ardent criticism. Innovation contains a self-fulfilling promise: that only innovation can provide us with a way to cope with innovation. This circularity is backed by past achievements and extends toward a fragile future, even while promising to transcend the present.

Cultures of Technology

Culture matters—this has been one of the most often-heard messages. It matters in its attempts to explain why economic opportunities have been seized in one country or region, and why economic failures have occurred in another. It matters not only for economic development, but also for political development. It promotes change—or impedes it (Lawrence and Huntington 2000). It matters when corporations with different organizational cultures merge or fail to do so. With organizations increasingly moving in global environments, they are well-advised to broaden their cultural range and to question the assumption that their concepts are universally valid. In the field of organizational learning, for instance, a shift has occurred toward a concept of organizational culture as the unit in which learning occurs. The culture of an organization is said to be pivotal to understanding how a particular organization adapts to ongoing changes. It shapes perceptions of past and current events. The emphasis is on shared conceptions of what needs to be learned, how it is to be learned, and why (Dierkes et al. 2001). Culture is understood here in its most encompassing sense: a shared scheme of interpretation that enables the organization to cope with change.

Culture matters—and indeed it permeates an enormously wide range of social activities. It binds together communities or sets them apart. It makes communities different from each other, shaping their interaction not only among members, but between the community and outsiders. It is linked to innovation in often unforeseeable ways in the sense that it can be predisposed to finding certain innovative solutions to a problem while eschewing other. In an interesting case study, the economic historian Avner Greif has analyzed the relationship between culture, innovation, and the institutional structure. Integrating game-theory with sociological concepts and basing his work on comparative historical material, he examines cultural factors that have led two premodern societies, one from the Arab and the other from the Latin world, to evolve along distinct trajectories of institutional structure. Based upon historical records from the late 11th century, Greif demonstrates that the two societies of medieval traders, the Genoese and the Maghribis, the latter, Jewish merchants living in a Muslim society, were both involved in mercantile relationships all over the Mediterranean. They employed comparable naval technology and traded in similar merchandise. The success of their trade depended to a large extent on their ability to mitigate the provision of services required for handling a merchant's goods abroad. A merchant could either provide these services himself or, as was most often the case, employ overseas agents to handle the merchandise, since this was a time-consuming endeavor. Employing agents was efficient, since it saved time and removed the risk of travel. Yet without supporting institutions, agency relations could not be established due to the potential of embezzlement.

Culture matters—since the Genoese society was much more individualistic, while the Maghribis were collectivistic. Their strategies (which Greif also analyzes in game-theoretical terms) differed accordingly. The results touch upon different patterns of wealth distribution and their consequences for the political organization of the society, as well as upon the way in which the two societies coped when they expanded their trade to areas previously inaccessible. The Genoese responded in an "integrated" manner, the Maghribis in a "segregated" manner. Both projected their cultural beliefs onto the new situation. But their cultural beliefs did not specify what the best response would be. The "segregated" response culminated in merchants from each society preferring to hire agents from their own society, while in the "integrated" response, there was no preference. Constrained by the same technology and environment and facing the same organizational problems, the two societies had different cultural heritages and social and political histories. In one case, however, collectivistic cultural beliefs led to an innovative response consisting in investments in information, segregation, and to a stable pattern of wealth distribution, while in the other case, individualistic cultural beliefs induced different kinds of enforcement mechanisms, a vertical social structure, a relatively low level of information, and to economic and social integration and wealth transfer to the relatively poor. In the end, both systems were efficient in the sense that they produced innovations, although in different ways, and each had to pay a price for its relative strengths and weaknesses. Nevertheless, Greif concludes, the individualism displayed by the Genoese medieval society may have cultivated the seeds that contributed to later economic and technological development and to the so-called rise of the West (Greif 1994).

To approach technology from a cultural perspective it is, therefore, at once self-evident and highly demanding: self-evident, because technology is one of the most consequential cultural practices to have evolved since the beginnings of humanity. The extension of human capacities that allowed humans to overcome and to extend their given biologic constraints, as well as those of the natural habitat in which they found themselves, is truly impressive. Merlin Donald has drawn attention to the rise of symbolic technologies, the invention and manipulation of external symbols that have changed the way in which we think, remember, and experience reality (Donald 2001). This rise of symbolic technologies has triggered a powerful cognitive transition (the first was the origin of language), liberating consciousness from the limitations of the brain's biologic memory system. Symbolic technologies have opened the gateway to allow the merging of symbolic virtuality with material reality. They are wired together in a distributed cognitive system that gives rise to cultural possibilities. Human conscious capacity, distributed over the entire society, is a resource that limits the rate at which culture can accumulate knowledge and determines what kinds of representational systems a culture can successfully construct and maintain.

But to approach technology from a cultural perspective is also highly demanding: highly demanding since it requires one to confront both technology's materiality and the cultural system of meaning with which technological practices are invested. Such a perspective raises questions as to the identity of the makers, controllers, facilitators, and shapers of technology. The enormous impact of today's information and communication technologies, including their powers of visualization, is linked to their dissemination throughout society. They have greatly facilitated the ongoing processes of globalization—with all of its downsides. New groups of users have gained access to these technologies and continue to take them in unexpected directions. The role of the nation-state as an advocate of technology is also in flux, although the state, by maintaining its monopoly over violence, remains a steadfast and generous supporter, especially of military technology. Globalization and its impact upon domestic arrangements also leads to a growing demand for transnational rules and regulations, which affect in turn the conditions under which cultures of technology are either stifled or allowed to flourish.

What is gained by conceiving of technology not just as an ensemble of artifacts or complex sociotechnical systems, but as *culture*? If we take the meaning of culture in its strictest anthropological sense—although there is no commonly agreed-upon definition of culture in anthropology either—we can say that culture does not exist independent of social interactions. Culture is about social relations with meanings attached to what people believe, do, and how they relate to each other and to their environment. Technological culture incudes technical artifacts as an integral part of this web of significance. The web of significance that human beings have spun themselves, and in which they are suspended, following Clifford Geertz's description (Geertz 1972), makes sense only when it is linked to human agency, intentions, interactions, results, and to the ensuing effects and transformations. Technology enters in an immensely practical way as a mediating object, acting upon social interactions and relationships and being acted upon. It does so by providing a "tight coupling of causally related elements" (Niklas Luhmann) rooted in their material and symbolic base. Technology may dispense with decisions, and it may replace the arduous process of consensus finding, because decisions have been taken before and have been transformed into such a "tight coupling of causally related elements." This is how technology works. Within the frame of these couplings, automatic, and hence predictable sequences, are guaranteed—but they still mediate some kind of social interaction or purpose. When the coupling is extended, the use and the power of symbolic technology comes from both their externalization and from being shared culturally across the multitude of minds, each dependent upon the other to further enhance the potential embodied by technology.

Cultures of technology are about arrangements. To speak about different cultures of technology breaks down the distinction between the material tool or its built-in technological efficiency, and the social organization, including the individual user and their social interactions. Cultures of technology are about shared meanings. Culture organizes practices. The processes and the range of ways in which this is done also matters. To focus on cultures of technology does not imply a neglect of the subtle impact that technology has on our lives, nor does it ignore the first steps in the genesis of emerging new technology. Rather, the emphasis is on what John Pickstone (in the alternative frame he has developed to take a fresh historical look across the entire spectrum of science, technology, and medicine), calls "ways of doing" (Pickstone 2001).

Technology works—and we expect it to work. It works on different levels and in different ways. They work through the tight or loose coupling of the elements that make up a technological system. They work through the ways in which people organize their work and through the division of labor in manufacturing or in service industries. They work by mediating social interaction. But they also work in a very powerful way by generating symbolic and cultural meanings. Any comprehensive account of technological innovation, as John Pickstone writes in this book, must allow for these meanings, including their supposed derivation from science. If we can see how the various elements of technology—from long-standing and usually traditional crafts, by way of systematic invention dating from about 1870 and demanding considerable social organization and education, to the present situation of high-tech, high-science complexity spreading across many sectors with the increasing use of computers at its base-fit together in history and our present, then we will have a good model for understanding technological innovation, including its cultural meaning.

Cultures of technology should therefore prepare us to understand where the quest for innovation comes from, pushing us forcefully to go far beyond any imagined "endless frontier." Innovation is no longer a goal, since it has, by its very nature, espoused a striving for the unpredictable and the unknown. Perhaps it has become a means—however, it can only constitute a tentative attempt to cope with the idea of a future that has become full of surprises.

Today, the modern management of risk, notwithstanding the many unresolved problems, has become highly professionalized and, as we have seen, is thriving in one sector that has transformed it into a business of its own, the management of financial markets. But technology, often lumped together indiscriminately with the concept of a unified science or seen as merely applied science, has become associated, if not tarnished, with the negative consequences they have also had on the social fabric of modern societies. The confidence in the achievement of sustainable technological progress is a precarious one, punctuated time and again by scandals involving the political management and regulation of risks associated with technological advances. The quest for ongoing innovation promises a way out. Its very open-endedness suggests a new flexibility and may point in the direction of improved and safe technology. It may gesture toward collective learning processes, which span the public and private domains and may bring with them social innovations of a kind as yet unknown.

The goal of this volume is to identify cultures of technology as a way of working across the entire societal spectrum, linking the technical intricacies with the requirements of the social and economic fabric of societies, uncovering the meanings that people attribute to how technology works, including how it affects their lives. They cover a wide range of human experience in the project of promoting certain cultures of technologies or confronting their consequences.

One part of this experience is gender-specific. Only the culture of war seems to be a human constant over time, although it also alters its manifestations and increases the power of its destructive force. As will become abundancy clear, speaking about cultures of technology never means speaking about technology alone. Admitting that technology can also be vulnerable reveals its entangled interdependence with the wider society—for better or for worse.

References

Arthur, Brian W. "Increasing Returns and the New World of Business." *Harvard Business Review* (July–August 1996): 1–10.

Beckert, Jens. *Beyond the Market. The Social Foundation of Economic Efficiency.* Princeton: Princeton University Press, 2002.

Bernstein, Peter L. *Against the Gods. The Remarkable Story of Risk.* New York: Wiley, 1996.

Branscomb, Lewis M. "Technological Innovation." In *International Encyclopedia of the Social & Behavioral Sciences*, edited by Neil J. Smelser and Paul B. Baltes, 5. Amsterdam: Science Direct, 2001.

Campbell, Donald T. "Variation and Selective Retention in Socio-Cultural Evolution." *General Systems* 14 (1969): 69–85.

———. "On the Conflicts Between Biological and Social Evolution and Between Psychology and Moral Tradition." *American Psychologist* (December 1975): 1103–1126.

Dierkes, Meinolf, Ariane Berthoin Antal, John Child, and Ikujiro Nonaka, eds., *Handbook of Organizational Learning and Knowledge.* Oxford: Oxford University Press, 2001.

Donald, Merlin. *A Mind So Rare: The Evolution of Human Consciousness.* New York: W. W. Norton & Company, 2001.

Geertz, Clifford. *Interpretation of Cultures.* New York: Basic Books, 1972.

Greif, Avner. "Cultural Beliefs and the Organization of Society: A Historical and Theoretical Reflection on Collectivist and Individualist Societies." *Journal of Political Economy* 102, no. 5 (1994): 912–950.

Gibbons, Michael, Camille Limoges, Helga Nowotny, Simon Schwartzman, Peter Scott, and Martin Trow. *The New Production of Knowledge: The Dynamics of Science and Research in Contemporary Societies.* London: Sage Publications, 1994.

Green, Stephen. "Negotiating with the Future: The Culture of Modern Risk in Global Financial Markets." *Environment and Planning D: Society a Space* 18 (2000): 77–89.

Hughes, Thomas P. *Rescuing Prometheus.* New York: Pantheon Books, 1998.

Latour, Bruno. *We Have Never Been Modern.* Boston: Harvard University Press, 1993.

Lawrence, Harrison E. and Samuel P. Huntington, eds. *Culture Matters: How Values Shape Human Progress.* New York: Basic Books, 2000.

Marx, Leo. "Technology: The Emergence of a Hazardous Concept." *Social Research 64*, no. 3 (1997): 965–988.

Meadows, Dennis L., Donella H. Meadows, Jørgen Randers, and William Behrens III. *The Limits to Growth.* New York: The Club of Rome, 1972.

Nelson, Richard R., ed. *National Innovation Systems: A Comparative Analysis.* New York: Oxford University Press, 1993.

Nowotny, Helga. "Vergangene Zukunft; Ein Blick zurück auf die Grenzen des Wachstums." In *Impulse geben—Wissen stiften. 40 Jahre Volkswagenstiftung,* edited by Michael Globig, 655–694. Göttingen: Vandenhoeck & Ruprecht, 2002.

———. "Wish Fulfilment and Its Discontents," *EMBO Reports 4,* no. 10 (2003): 917–920.

Nowotny, Helga, ed. *Cultures of Technology and the Quest for Innovation.* New York: Berghahn Books, 2006.

Nowotny, Helga and Peter Scott. "Mode of Knowledge Production." In *Elgar Encyclopedia of Interdisciplinarity and Transdisciplinarity,* edited by Frédéric Darbellay, 338–342. Cheltenham: Edward Elgar Publishing, 2024.

Pickstone, John V. *Ways of Knowing: A New History of Science, Technology, and Medicine.* Manchester: Manchester University Press, 2000 and Chicago: University of Chicago Press, 2001.

Rabinow, Paul. *Making PCR: A Story of Biotechnology.* Chicago: The University of Chicago Press, 1996.

Rosenberg, Nathan and L. E. Birdzell Jr. *How the West Grew Rich: The Economic Transformation of the Industrial World.* New York: Basic Books, 1985.

Schumpeter, Joseph A. *The Theory of Economic Development. An Inquiry into Profits, Capital, Credit, Interest, and the Business Cycle.* Cambridge, Mass.: Transaction Publishers, 1934 (original: *Therie der wirtschaftlichen Entwicklung.* Leipzig, Germany, 1912).

Shackle, G. L. S. *Decision, Order, and Time in Human Affairs.* Cambridge: Cambridge University Press, 1969.

Webster, Daniel. *The Writings and Speeches of Daniel Webster.* Boston: Little, Brown and Company, 1903.

III.

Introduction to "*Mode 2*" Revisited: *The New Production of Knowledge*[*]

This paper revisits the original thesis about *The New Production of Knowledge*, published in 1994, and its successor volume, *Re-Thinking Science*, from 2001. The original thesis provoked a lively discussion and soon became known under the phrase of "Mode 2." In contrast to the old paradigm of scientific discovery ("Mode 1"), the new production of knowledge is socially distributed, application-oriented, trans-disciplinary, and subject to multiple accountabilities. "Mode 2" was warmly espoused by those who had something to gain from it. These were the policymakers and research funders struggling to create better links between science and innovation, as well as researchers in professional disciplines like management and those in newer universities or at the margins of the old academic disciplinary hierarchy. Predictably, those with most to lose were skeptical, including researchers in established disciplines and institutions

---

[*] Originally published in Helga Nowotny, Peter H. Scott and Michael Gibbons, "Introduction: *'Mode 2' Revisited: The New Production of Knowledge*," *Minerva* 41, no. 3 (September 2003): 179–194, https://doi.org/10.1023/A:1025505528250.

who feared that the quality of science would be eroded and their own authority imperiled if more explicit links between research and innovation would take over.

Re-Thinking Science was a response to the criticisms raised and a further, substantial development of the argument. The successor volume articulates more sharply the relationship between "science" and "society" by identifying the key changes taking place in society and introduced the "context of application" as crucial for the operation of "Mode 2." It concluded that "Mode 2" should be seen as an ongoing project that emphasizes the emergence of more open knowledge production systems by fluid forms of knowledge that are inter- and transdisciplinary, seeking to enhance the problem-solving capacity that "science" can offer to "society" when it listens to "society speaking back."

From today's vantage point, "Mode 2" has largely been vindicated and has been absorbed in the ongoing transformation of unsettling disciplinary science. The increasing number and variety of stakeholders, from research bureaucracies to potential users, are aligned towards moving research in the direction of innovation, impact, and output. "Mode 2" was not the only concept following the dynamics of science beyond disciplinary boundaries. The "Triple Helix" links the scientific, political, and economic systems while "post-normal science" emphasizes problem-solving strategies when "facts are uncertain, values in dispute, stakes high and decisions urgent."

Reflecting on the usefulness of the term "knowledge production," which opens scientific research towards wider society. Peter Scott and I have highlighted two core beliefs about the nature of science that have remained highly influential in both normative and operational terms. The first belief asserts that excellent science is best produced under the least constrained conditions, with fundamental science proving "The Usefulness of Useless Knowledge," epitomized in Abram Flexner's manifesto. It retains its scientific appeal, affirmed by the establishment and success of the European Research Council. The other belief into the necessity of disciplines for determining and upholding the quality of research is losing ground. Recent attempts to reform research assessment and developments like the Open Science movement and other measures to grapple with the flood of publications, including fakes, are gaining momentum. The impact of AI and Big Data is rapidly advancing, and answers are needed that enable research to sustain its critical function in society. The term "knowledge production" offers a context in which recent trends can be helpfully framed and better understood (Nowotny, Scott, and Gibbons 2001).

❒❑❒

Introduction

Nine years ago, six authors published *The New Production of Knowledge: The Dynamics of Science and Research in Contemporary Societies* (Gibbons et al. 1994). Reviews were mixed. Some philosophers, historians, and sociologists science regarded the argument in the book as either simplistic or banal perhaps both), while science policy analysts worried about the empirical evidence for the trends it identified (or argued that these trends were new). However, the book's broad thesis —that the production of knowledge and the process of research were being radically transformed—struck a chord of recognition among both researchers and policy.

Of course, like all theses that gain a certain popularity (and notoriety) it was radically simplified, collapsed into a single phrase—"Mode 2." The old paradigm of scientific discovery ("Mode 1")—characterized by the hegemony of theoretical or, at any rate, experimental science, by an internally driven taxonomy of disciplines and by the autonomy of scientists and their host institutions, the universities, was being superseded by a new paradigm of knowledge production ("Mode 2"), which was socially distributed, application-oriented, transdisciplinary, and subject to multiple accountabilities.

Those with most to gain from such a thesis espoused it most warmly—politicians and civil servants struggling to create better mechanisms to link science with innovation, researchers in professional disciplines such as management struggling to wriggle out from under the condescension of more established, and more "academic," disciplines, and researchers in newer universities, other non-university higher education institutions or outside the academic, and scientific, systems strictly defined. Those with most to lose were most skeptical—researchers in those established disciplines and institutions who feared that the quality of science would be eroded if these levelling ideas gained political currency and that their own autonomy would be curtailed if more explicit links were established between research and innovation.

Both reactions were predictable. A generation ago, Thomas Kuhn's *The Structure of Scientific Revolutions* aroused far more interest among social scientists, even humanists—who not only felt a shock of recognition in his account of paradigm shift but also saw that it could enhance the legitimacy of their disciplines—than among natural scientists, who saw Kuhn's companion idea of incommensurability as a threat not only to universal, or "objective," truth but also to progressive experimentally based research (Kuhn 1970). His own discipline, physics, was most resistant of all to his ideas (Gutting 1980).

However, in the case of *The New Production of Knowledge* there was a new twist. The "Mode 2" thesis, however simplified, was recognizably derived from the argument presented in the book. So as authors we could not object. Our critics may even have regarded us as hoist by our own petard, because inherent in the very notion of Mode 2, or socially distributed knowledge, is the idea that it cannot be authoritatively encoded in traditional forms of scholarly publication. If nurse researchers pounced on "Mode 2" to reduce their subordination to medical research, or if global accountancy companies placed "Mode 2" at the heart of newly established "Centers for Business Knowledge" —both of which are actual examples—who were we, the authors, to complain? We had fallen into our own post-modern trap.

It was partly to resist this collapse into relativism (and over-simplification of the argument), partly to answer the valid criticisms of that argument and partly to develop our broader thesis that the present three authors wrote a second book *Re-Thinking Science: Knowledge and the Public in an Age of Uncertainty* (Nowotny, Scott and Gibbons 2001). Yet the difficulty remains—how to describe and defend in traditional academic discourse ("Mode 1" in our own terminology) ideas that attempt to analyze how that discourse is being transcended ("Mode 2"). "Mode 2" is not only a concept, inherently open to manipulation or exploitation by others (even in ways of which we may disapprove); it is also a project, an example of the social distribution of knowledge which it seeks to describe.

This article cannot hope to resolve this difficulty. Instead, we hope it will contribute to the continuing debate about the future of knowledge production. It is divided into four sections: (1) a description of trends in science policy and tendencies within the research enterprise out of which our analysis first arose, and which have intensified in the past eight years; (2) a summary of the arguments first presented in *The New Production of Knowledge*; (3) an account of how these arguments have been extended and elaborated (and, perhaps, modified) in *Re-Thinking Science*; and (4) a brief speculation about next steps, because our thesis is highly reflexive and closure of the argument is not possible.

The Changing Research Environment

The nature of the research process is being transformed, and this transformation has many separate elements. Scholars disagree about their respective novelty and intensity. However, three trends are generally accepted to be significant – (a) the 'steering' of research priorities, (b) the commercialization of research, and (c) the accountability of science. These and other trends, or changes in practice, have given rise to new discourses of science and research.

a) The Steering of Research Priorities

The first element in the transformation of research is the increasing desire to "steer" priorities. This operates at several levels:

(i) The supranational level: The best example of this perhaps are the successive European Community Framework programs. These programs have attempted to shape research priorities and build research capacity to meet identified social and economic needs. On the whole, these efforts have been supported by the research community because the Framework programs, inevitably, have been broad in their scope, and consequently few areas have been categorically excluded and because these programs have provided genuinely additional resources;

(ii) The national level: Although highly prescriptive, research and development programs (for example, those funded by ministries of health, defense or agriculture) have existed for some time, there has been a growing tendency for all ministries to develop dedicated research programs. These programs, rather confusingly, both focus on short-term political agendas and attempt to develop long-term research capacity. There has been a tendency for "Foresight" exercises, which initially attempted to predict future research needs in a relatively open and speculative way, to be succeeded by more directive approaches as industry and trade ministries have attempted to identify both areas of international excellence and of inadequate research capacity within the context of global economic competitiveness; and

(iii) The system level: In many countries, Research Councils have increasingly adopted more proactive (or top-down) identification of research priorities in place of the essentially reactive (or bottom-up) policies whereby the best research proposals, as identified by peer review, are funded. Much greater emphasis is now placed on thematic programs. Although typically broad in their scope, these programs are often the product of an awkward—and unstable—compromise between "political" goals, promising science and available research capacity. In a similar way, universities have begun to manage their research priorities more aggressively rather than simply providing a support environment.

b) The Commercialization of Research

The second element is the commercialization of research, although this label can be misleading; engaged research may be a more accurate description. This has taken two main forms. First, as the public funding of research has become less adequate, researchers have increasingly turned to alternative sources of funding. Secondly, universities (and similar organizations) have become more aware of the value of the intellectual property generated by their research. More attention, and anxiety, has focused on the first than the second—perhaps wrongly. The available public funding for research is inevitably outrun by the sheer fecundity of research potential, although this is not an argument for abandoning efforts to increase public funding. The funding of research has always come from a plurality of sources; arguably this contributes to the diversity—and creativity—of the research system. Of greater concern perhaps is the tendency of government to define its role in research funding in quasi-commercial rather than fiduciary terms. This attempt to align public policy with market priorities in research policy—creating what are, in effect, public-private partnerships —is likely to reduce diversity and creativity.

The second aspect, the determination to exploit "intellectual property," raises greater concern. The motives of universities and similar organizations are obvious enough. Public expenditure on higher education and research generally has failed to keep pace with costs, and universities have been encouraged to develop alternative sources of income. With the emergence of a Knowledge Society, knowledge "products," many of which are derived from university research, are increasingly valued, not in terms of their long-term potential, but in terms of immediate market return. However understandable the motives, seeking to exploit "intellectual property" has two important consequences.

First, by raising the question of who "owns" this property (i.e., the individual researcher or research team, the research community, or the institution) and then negotiating their respective shares, the exploitation of intellectual property transforms the organizational character of the university. Second, the exploitation of "intellectual property" challenges the idea (ideal?) of science as a public good. This raises awkward issues. One is commercial confidentiality. If "intellectual property" is valuable, it cannot be given away "freely" by open publication in peer-reviewed journals or at scientific conferences open to all. However, the quality of science is largely determined by its exposure to refutation and counter-argument. This process becomes much more difficult if the circulation of research findings is restricted.

c) The Accountability of Science

The third element in the transformation of research is the growing emphasis placed on the management of research—and, in particular, efforts to evaluate its effectiveness and assess its quality. A good example is the Research Assessment Exercise (RAE) conducted by the higher education funding councils in England, Scotland and Wales, most recently in 2001 (Scott 2000). In the RAE no (overt) attempt is made to influence the kind of research that gets done, in terms of its themes, concepts or methodologies. In practice, of course, the notions of international and national "significance" on which the RAE relies as a measurement criterion are not value-free; in all subjects there are prestigious themes, preferred concepts and preferred methodologies. But, as far as possible, the RAE attempts to include—and so to assess—all styles of research by adopting an all-encompassing definition of research. The funding councils also try to make the whole process as transparent as possible by publishing the detailed criteria used by each panel of assessors, by identifying their members, providing (limited) feedback on the grades awarded by these panels.

Important questions have been raised by the RAE. No measurement system, however scrupulously used, can fail to affect the behavior of that which it seeks to measure. The influence of the RAE on the behavior of individual researchers, research groups, departments, subjects and institutions has been manifold. Some resumes have amounted to cynical game-playing. But such game-playing—"star" researchers playing the transfer market like footballers, artificial or unrepresentative "entries" being contrived and so on—can be anticipated and, to some extent, discounted, although rule-changes tend to lag behind the abuses they are designed to combat (five years behind in the case of the RAE). A more serious consideration is the distortions produced and the hierarchies reinforced by the taxonomy of the assessment process itself, notably the demarcations between units-of-assessment. Interdisciplinary research has to be clumsily disaggregated, while truly creative research in the borderlands between disciplines is devalued. A third criticism is that RAE-type accountability and/or research management mechanisms have encouraged researchers to espouse industry-style production. It is said to be safer to deliver predictable (and second-best?) results on time than ground-breaking research, late.

To focus too closely on the RAE is perhaps unnecessary. The same principles are at work in many other contexts. During the past decade there has been a remarkable intensification of the associated processes of audit, assessment and evaluation, which has given rise to the suggestion that we now live in an "Audit Society" (having sinuous but suggestive links with the Knowledge Society) (Power 1997). These processes are at work at every level within the research system—within the research team, as it evaluates the contributions of its individual members; in departments as they seek to maximize their research performance; and in institutions, as they struggle to manage their overall research effort, as well as in funding councils and government departments.

This is a key point. It is a mistake to imagine that accountability is being forced on universities and other research institutions by hostile external forces, even if the mutual trust once rooted in the collusion of political, administrative and academic élites has been eroded; the processes of assessment and accountability have been deeply internalized—and, at the same time, have moved from the arena of professional (or collegial) responsibility to the domain of organizational (and managerial) competence. Power has theorized these processes in interesting ways as "rituals of verification."

A New Discourse of Science?

As a result of these and other trends, the research that is variously described as "pure," "blue-skies," fundamental or disinterested, is now a minority preoccupation—even in universities. In Britain, Research Councils and RAE panels now include "user" representatives alongside more traditional scientific peers. Detailed impact studies and lengthy evaluations have become routine. "Knowledge" is now regarded not as a public good, but rather as "intellectual property," which is produced, accumulated and traded like other goods and services in the

Knowledge Society. In the process, a new language has been invented —a language of application, relevance, contextualization, reach-out, technology transfer, knowledge management.

Efforts to develop this new language—by which to describe the transformation of research, to map its new concepts, and to create a new discourse—have produced an extensive body of literature. The includes a literature of "regret," which treats this transformation as inimical to the production of high-quality research (as well as potential threat to free thought and the open society). In the United Kingdom, the Campaign for Academic Freedom and Democracy has been articulate, and aggressive, in representing this point of view, but it is a view that is also shared among academic scientists. There is also a new literature of "modernization," emphasizing the importance of research within the Knowledge Society—and the need to align research priorities more closely with social, economic, and political goals. In Britain, successive White Papers—typically with titles such as "Realizing Our Potential"—and the various Foresight exercises, reflect this second point of view. Neither, however, attempt a deeper analysis of changes in how knowledge is produced, validated and disseminated. Both tend to regard the inner core of the research enterprise as essentially unchanged, and unchanging.

Finally, there is a literature of empirical investigation. For example, the Institute for Scientific Information (ISI) in Philadelphia has used large-scale datasets to generate citation indices which, despite their imperfections, have increased our understanding of the dominant modes of scientific production. Research groups, such as the Science Policy Research Unit (SPRU) at the University of Sussex, have done valuable work on changes in patterns of scientific publication—examining, for example, the trend towards multi-institutional authorship (including many more non-university institutions, notably in the health sector) and the growth of so-called "grey" literature (Hicks and Katz 1996). Finally, there is a literature of theoretical speculation. Some examples, such as John Ziman's recent book, have attempted to re-justify the traditional autonomy of science (Ziman 2000). Others, such as Henry Etzkowitz's conceptualization of the science-industry-government relationship as a "triple helix" have embraced, and sought to explain, a new research paradigm (Etzkowitz and Leydesdorff 1997). Others again, such as Katrin Knorr-Cetina's work on the dynamics cultures, have adopted an intermediate position (Knorr-Cetina 1999).

The New Production of Knowledge

Both *The New Production of Knowledge* and *Re-Thinking Science* were written as reflective essays rather than empirical studies. Their purpose was as much to address the need to invent a new language of research, as to offer a detailed analysis of the trends we have just described. In *The New Production of Knowledge*, the notion of "Mode 2" knowledge production was introduced—and contrasted with "Mode 1" research. "Mode 2" knowledge production has a number of characteristics:

(i) "Mode 2" knowledge is generated within the context of application. This is different from the process of application by which "pure" science, generated in theoretical/experimental environments, is applied; any technology is "transferred"; and knowledge is subsequently "managed." The context of application, in contrast, describes the total environment in which scientific problems arise, methodologies are developed, outcomes are disseminated and uses are defined.

(ii) The second characteristic is trans-disciplinarity, by which is meant the mobilization of a range of theoretical perspectives and practical methodologies to solve problems. But, unlike inter- or multi-disciplinarity, it is not necessarily derived from pre-existing disciplines, nor does it always contribute to the formation of new disciplines. The creative act lies just as much in the capacity to mobilize and manage these perspectives and methodologies, their "external" orchestration, as in the development of new theories or conceptualizations, or the refinement of research methods, the "internal" dynamics of scientific creativity. In other words, "Mode 2" knowledge is embodied in the expertise of individual researchers and research teams as much as, or possibly more than, it is encoded in conventional research products such as journal articles or even patents;

(iii) The third characteristic of "Mode 2" is the much greater diversity of the sites at which knowledge is produced, and in the types of knowledge producted. The first phenomenon, it can be argued, is not especially new. Research communities have always been "virtual" communities that cross national (and cultural) boundaries. But in "Mode 2," their dynamics have been transformed. Once interaction within these communities was limited by the constraints, both physical (the ability to meet) and technical (letters and telephones); now, as a result of advances in information and communication, technologies interaction is unconstrained—and instantaneous. The orderly hierarchies imposed by these "old" technologies of interaction are being eroded by this communicative free-for-all. This shift has been intensified by the second phenomenon—the fact that these research communities now have open frontiers—which has allowed many new kinds of "knowledge" organizations—such as think-tanks, management consultants, and activist groups, to join the research game.

(iv) The fourth characteristic of "Mode 2" knowledge is that it is highly reflexive. The research process can no longer be characterized as an "objective" investigation of the natural (or social) world, or as a cool and reductionist interrogation of arbitrarily defined "others." Instead, it has become a dialogic process, an intense (and perhaps endless) "conversation" between research actors and research subjects—to such an extent that the basic vocabulary of research (who, whom, what, how) is in danger of losing its significance. As a result, traditional notions of "accountability" have had to be radically revised. The consequences (predictable and unintended) of new knowledge cannot be regarded as being "outside" the research process because problem-solving environments influence topic-choice and research-design as well end-uses;

(v) The fifth characteristic is seen in novel forms of quality control. First, in "Mode 2" knowledge, scientific "peers" can no longer be reliably identified, because there is no longer a stable taxonomy of codified disciplines from which "peers" can be drawn. Second, reductionist forms of quality control cannot easily be applied to much more broadly-framed research questions; the research "game" is being joined by more and more players—not simply a wider and more eclectic range of "producers," but also orchestrators, brokers, disseminators, and users. Third, and most disturbingly, clear and unchallengable criteria, by which to determine quality may no longer be available. Instead, we must learn to live with multiple definitions of quality, a fact that seriously complicates (even compromises) the processes of discrimination, prioritization and selectivity on which policy-makers and funding agencies have come to rely.

In *The New Production of Knowledge*, the idea of "Mode 2" knowledge, with these five characteristics, was developed in a number of concrete contexts. The first was the commercialization of research. This provided a more nuanced account than either of the two standard accounts — characterizing commercialization as a threat to scientific autonomy (and so, ultimately, to scientific quality); and as the means by which research is revitalized in both priorities and uses, and in the resources it commands (because public funding of research is inherently both constraining and insufficient).

The second context was the development of mass higher education. The great increase in the number of students over the past half century, and the equally spectacular expansion of research, have often seemed uneasy bedfellows. Between 1945 and the mid 1970s, the former initially enhanced the resource base for the latter, but in recent years, these two elements have become increasingly competitive. More seriously, mass access and high-quality research have come to be driven by, and to address, different value systems. But this may partly be explained by the persistence of a traditional —"Mode 1"— account of research. Within the context of "Mode 2," these tensions are reduced, and new synergies are apparent between the democratization of higher education and the wider social distribution of knowledge production.

The third context was the role of the humanities in the production of knowledge. The conventional view is that the humanities are the most detached disciplines, furthest removed from the turmoil of application and contextualization. Their "uses" are almost entirely internalized. Our account in *The New Production of Knowledge* challenged that view. Instead we saw the humanities as the most engaged of all disciplines, not simply because they flow through into the culture industry (for example, through novels or popular history), but because they comfortably (and inevitably) embody notions of reflexivity which the natural, and even the social, sciences distrust.

The fourth context was globalization. Not only has "knowledge," in the form of world brands and massive (and instantaneous) data flows, become the key resource in the global economy, "scientific" knowledge more narrowly defined has also become more highly integrated and distributed. The idea of "Mode 2" knowledge, in our view, is a useful tool to unlock some of these apparently contradictory phenomena. For example, the tension between modernity (Enlightenment values and scientific culture) and modernization (the application of science and technology) becomes much less of a problem if a "Mode 2" perspective is adopted.

The fifth and sixth contexts to which we attempted to apply the idea of "Mode 2" were the least well developed. They were, first, the potential re-configuration of institutions that flowed from the wider distribution and greater reflexivity of knowledge production; and, second, the management of "Mode 2" knowledge. These are key issues. The modern world is populated by expert institutions, which are not only essential for the advancement of social and technical progress and professional careers, but also shape personal and group identities and influence both the constitution and the uses of knowledge. Similarly, the production of knowledge, however widely distributed, however transdisciplinary, however heterogeneous, however reflexive, has to be "managed." More choices have to be made more urgently about scientific priorities. Although the explosion of choice may make it more difficult to aggregate them into, or shape them within, the framework of planned programs, this does not mean that the problem of management has disappeared. Clearly "Mode 2" knowledge must be managed in new ways. These are themes to which we intend to return in a third book.

Re-Thinking Science

The New Production of Knowledge provoked a lively debate. The argument presented in the book was criticized on a number of grounds. To some, it amounted to little more than a legitimization of malignant trends — in particular, the subordination of research to market and political agendas on the mistaken assumption that scientific breakthroughs could be predicted and therefore planned (Ziman 1996). To others, the argument was not underpinned by adequate evidence; critics argued that the characteristics of knowledge production summed up by the "Mode 2" label were neither as significant nor as novel as we had suggested. Other critics pointed out that, although we made much of the wider social distribution of knowledge and, therefore, of the more intense engagement between science and society, no real attempt was made to discuss the dynamics of society, which were treated as an unproblematic given. Some accepted the accuracy of our account, but insisted that it described social and political epiphenomena; the core of science remained inviolate. Finally, others saw *The New Production of Knowledge* as offering a postmodern vision of research (David 1996).

Re-Thinking Science was an attempt both to respond to these critics and, more substantially, to develop the argument. Some of these criticisms were well-founded—in particular the last two. However, the idea of "Mode 2" was never intended to be a new-fangled label for applied science or programmatic research; by questioning the linearity and predictability of the research process, it called into question definitions of applied as well as pure research. Neither *The New Production of Knowledge* nor *Re-Thinking Science* was intended to be an empirical study. The aim of this second book was not simply to answer critics of the first. Rather, it was to take the two most substantial critiques and, by addressing them, offer a more theoretical account of the argument advanced in *The New Production of Knowledge*. First, the relationships between "science" and "society" were articulated more clearly to give substance to the twin notions of "science speaking to society" and "society speaking back to science." The second book attempted to identify the key changes taking place in society. In the 1970s, these were confidently described in the language of industrial society. This assumed a post-industrialism in which knowledge accessible to (almost) all would replace physical, energy and financial resources rationed to the rich and in which the rough edges of ideological conflict would be smoothed away. Knowledge would create prosperity. In the past quarter-century this optimistic vision has been superseded by dark images of a society in which risks have remorselessly accumulated and new hegemonic "networks" have emerged.

Re-Thinking Science attempted to steer between optimists and pessimists, arguing instead that the great sub-systems of modernity (State, Market, Culture—and Science), once clearly partitioned, were becoming increasingly transgressive. This fuzziness helped to create the transaction spaces in which "Mode 2" knowledge developed (and also, perhaps, the new social movements). The second book concentrated on four key characteristics which, it was argued, were evident both in society and science. These were (i) the generation of uncertainty/ies, which reduces the possibility of post-positivistic planning—in both arenas; (ii) the trend towards self-organization, which is intimately related to the growth of reflexivity—again in both domains; (iii) the emergence of new forms of "economic rationality," according to which, as in any "futures" market, the potential of science is measured by its immanent rather than instrumental value; and (iv) the re-constitution of time/space of which the revolution in information and communication technology is one aspect.

Second, the assertion in *The New Production of Knowledge* that "Mode 2" knowledge was produced in a "context of application," was refined into a more developed argument about different forms of contextualization, so removing any possible doubt about a facile identification between such knowledge and applied research. Three forms of contextualization were examined. The first was "weak contextualization." Counter-intuitively, perhaps, national R&D programs are a good example because, to succeed, they must simplify both. The second was contextualization in the "middle range," in which the majority of "Mode 2" knowledge production is clustered. Here, so-called "trading zones," transaction spaces, and what we labelled "Mode-2 objects" play a crucial role in determining a form of contextualization in which local contingencies shape synergy and potential. The third was "strong contextualization," where powerful reflexive articulations between science and society were at work. This may take highly-specific forms, or relate to the interaction between the world of ideas and much wider social movements, such as feminism or environmentalism.

The third way in which we developed a more theoretical account of "Mode 2" was in arguing that this new knowledge form was not merely a secondary phenomenon, contingent on "Mode 1" science, as some critics had suggested. Three pieces of evidence were offered in support of this claim. The first was that "Mode 2," especially in its trans-disciplinary dimension, could make a fundamental contribution to the development not only of new methodologies but also of new concepts and theories. The failure to recognize this contribution probably arose from the fact that it was not encoded in disciplinary frameworks or embodied in familiar research products such as journal articles. The second piece of evidence was that the epistemological core of science, the values in which it is ultimately rooted, may be a mirage; *often* it was empty (as, for example, when scientific ideas are absorbed by non-host cultures, predominantly as technical artefacts without regard to their original normative significance) or, more usually, when it is crowded with competing epistemologies. The third was that reliable knowledge, the traditional goal of scientific inquiry, is no longer (self?) sufficient in the more open knowledge environments that are now emerging; knowledge also needs to be "socially robust," because its validity is no longer determined solely, or predominantly, by narrowly circumscribed scientific communities, but by much wider communities of engagement comprising knowledge producers, disseminators, traders and users.

Finally, two new ideas were introduced. The first, related to the fuller explication of contextualization, was the concept of the *agora*. This archaism was deliberately chosen to embrace the political arena and the marketplace — and to go beyond both. The *agora* is the problem-generating and problem-solving environment in which the contextualization of knowledge production takes place. It is populated not only by arrays of competing "experts," and the organizations and institutions through which knowledge is generated and traded, but also variously jostling "publics." It is not simply a political or commercial arena in which research priorities are identified and funded, nor an arena in which research findings are disseminated, traded and used. The *agora* is a domain of primary knowledge production — through which people enter the research process, and where "Mode 2" knowledge is embodied in people and projects. The role of controversies in realizing scientific potential is also played out in the *agora*.

The second new idea introduced in *Re-Thinking Science* is that of the context of application. This was taken to be one of the key characteristics of "Mode 2" in *The New Production of Knowledge*. But to the extent that the context of application seems silently to reinforce notions of hierarchy and linearity, and to suggest that positivistic predictions of applicability are possible, it could be regarded as dangerously misleading. Instead, against a background of inherent uncertainty about the future state of knowledge, from which scientific potential was derived, it is necessary to reach beyond the knowable context of application, towards the unknowable context of implication. Here knowledge-seekers have to reach out and anticipate reflexively the implications of research processes.

Re-Thinking Science attempted to fill some of the gaps in the argument in *The New Production of Knowledge*—notably, the absence of an adequate social theory, and the lack of a convincing refutation of the claim that "Mode 2" knowledge is a secondary activity. However, there is need to systematically explore the implications of these ideas for systems and institutions in general, which will be the focus of the authors' next work. Closure of the "Mode 2" debate is neither possible nor desirable. The project has many characteristics of the much more open knowledge production systems that is attempting to analyse —wide social distribution, trans-disciplinarity, the need for social robustness, and the creative potential of controversies.

This special issue of *Minerva* is its own *agora*, containing five articles that address themes emerging from both books (and other interventions and contributions to the wider debate). In the first, John de la Mothe discusses the impact of more subtle readings of the process of innovation on policy organizations and policy behavior, and therefore addresses one of the shortcomings in our analysis. Next, Olle Edqvist describes the layers of Swedish research policy laid down in the 1940s, 1960s, and 1990s as embodying three different models of science —as the motor of progress; problem-solver; and strategic opportunity. In his view, "Mode 2," or distributed knowledge production, has been the historical norm; it is "Mode 1," or academic science, that is the recent interloper. In the third article, Sheila Jasanoff argues that it is necessary to increase civic participation in the governance of science to compensate for the erosion of the authority of technical experts, and urges the adoption of what she calls "technologies of humility," which engage the human subject as both active agent and source of knowledge and insight. Her argument is a more eloquent extension of our account of the *agora* as a site of knowledge production.

In the fourth article, Dominique Pestre asserts that the arguments in *The New Production of Knowledge* and *Re-Thinking Science* do not stress sufficiently the extent to which the evolution science and society, analysed in these two books, are the result of political and social choices. He is particularly interested in alternatives to what he regards as over-deterministic accounts. The neglect of power relationships we acknowledge to be one of the most significant weaknesses in both our books, and Pestre's account helps to remedy this weakness. Marilyn Strathern extends these arguments into new, anthropological territory by discussing to what extent "society" can be described in sufficiently robust terms so that it can become a reference point, or counter-point, for "science." Although in *Re-Thinking Science* we attempted to offer a more subtle account of "society," Strathern's article demonstrates the scale and scope of the work that remains to be done.

References

David, Paul. "Science Reorganized? Postmodern Visions of Science and the Curse of Success." Proceedings of the 2nd International Symposium on Research Funding, Ottawa (1996): 191–136.

Etzkowitz, Henry and Loet Leydesdorff, eds. *Universities and the Global Knowledge Economy: a Triple Helix of University-Industry-Government Relations*, London: Pinter, 1997.

Gibbons, Michael, Camille Limoges, Helga Nowotny, Simon Schwartzman, Peter Scott and Martin Trow. *The New Production of Knowledge: The Dynamics of Science and Research in Contemporary Societies*. London: Sage, 1994.

Gutting, Gary ed. *Paradigms and Revolutions: Applications and Appraisals of Thomas Kuhn's Philosophy of Science*. Notre Dame: University of Notre Dame Press, 1980.

Hicks, Diana and J. Sylvan Katz. "Science Policy for a Highly Collaborative Science System." *Science and Public Policy* 23 (February 1996): 39–44.

Knorr-Cetina, Karin. *Epistemic Cultures: How the Sciences Make Knowledge*. Cambridge MA: Harvard University Press, 1999.

Kuhn, Thomas. *The Structure of Scientific Revolutions* (International Encyclopedia of Unified Science, vol. 2, number 2). Chicago: Chicago University Press, 1970.

Nowotny, Helga, Peter Scott and Michael Gibbons. *Re-Thinking Science: Knowledge and the Public in an Age of Uncertainty*. Cambridge: Polity Press, 2001.

Power, Michael. *The Audit Society: Rituals of Verification*. Oxford: Oxford University Press, 1997.

Scott, Peter. "The Impact of the Research Assessment Exercise on the Quality of British Science and Scholarship." *Anglistik* 1 (2000): 129–143.

Ziman, John. "Is Science Losing its Objectivity?" *Nature* 382 (1996): 751–754.

——. *Real Science: What it Is, and What it Means*. Cambridge: Cambridge University Press, 2000.

IV.

On the Changing Experience of Time: Eigenzeit. Revisited[*]

In 2014, I gave a keynote lecture at the Haus der Kulturen in Berlin on the occasion of an event called "100 Years of the Present" commemorating the beginning of WW1 and the temporal changes it induced. I had been asked specifically to reflect on my book *Eigenzeit*, published twenty-five years earlier, that had been a source of inspiration for the event. I began with how I was drawn into studying the topic of time which, once you start, never leaves you. For many contemporaries, a constant experience of time is its acceleration. This is not the direct result of new technologies that only mediate the multiple social interactions and inbuilt contradictions in social networks that are expanded as well as compressed through technologies. We cannot experience time directly, except through the temporal conflicts to which we are exposed. We expect to master simultaneity but are overwhelmed by the complexity it generates.

---

[*] Originally published in Helga Nowotny, "Eigenzeit. Revisited," in *An Orderly Mess* (Budapest: Central European University Press, 2017), 61–95.

Acceleration has become a feature also of human intervention into the living world, from biotechnologies to the destruction of the natural environment.

What I had not included a quarter of a century ago were the different time scales which we confront today through climate change, the processes of digitalization and the availability of big data. The speed of processing data and other inherent temporal features changes our sense of time. The past is indiscriminately recorded and thus homogenized, losing focus. Attention has become a scarce resource, reawakening the longing for the now. Digital technologies alter the experience of *Eigenzeit* through the abundance of apps at our instantaneous disposition. *Medial Eigenzeit*, as I called it, seemingly fulfills many dreams, but it is caught in an existential contradiction with lifetime, the aging processes of mind and body and its biological, emotional, and cognitive demands. I conclude by recalling what I had written in 1989 about the future intruding into the present which becomes an extended present, a diagnosis that has fully been affirmed. Yet, it also renders the concept of the future, and our ability to imagine it, more precarious.

Looking back ten years later, this essay holds up well when compared with the most significant changes that have since occurred. I have further expanded my observations and the analysis of digital time in *Life in the Digital Time Machine* (Nowotny 2020). However, and foremost, it is the concept of the future that continues to occupy and preoccupy my work. Partly, I have dealt with it in *The Cunning of Uncertainty*. My worries come from what I see as a shrinking of our capabilities to collectively imagine a future that goes beyond a bland extension of the digital present. Moreover, digital technologies, as I analyzed ten years ago, bring the past into the present while flattening and homogenizing it. The past is thus deprived of depth and context, and we lose the ability to connect it to the problems that we face in the present.

❒❑❒

Eigenzeit was published in the memorable year 1989. It is a very personal book, whose growth at the time followed the temporal rhythm of my life. In writing the book I was aiming for a social-science based diagnosis of current shifts in the meaning of the concept of time, of exposure to, and experience of time. I wanted to report on the contemporary experience people had with time and to analyze the conflicts emerging from it. I observed how the boundaries between private and public time began to blur in everyday life and was fascinated by the gradual absorption of the category of a distant future by what I called the extended present.

Everywhere I looked I stumbled upon those technologies that alter our perception of time in the most immediate and visible way: the new information and communication technologies. *Eigenzeit* set out to demonstrate the qualitative changes in the individual perception of time and the corresponding experience in their manifold connections to the structuration society imposes on time. Technologies played an important role throughout but the same was true for the globally virulent economic and political processes that added a new dimension to the nexus between power and time.

Why did I choose time as a topic? It all started early in 1973. At that time my then considerably younger self underwent an abrupt transition into a new phase of life. From a hectic professional routine compounded by a turbulent private situation, I found myself transported from one day to the next to serenely idyllic Cambridge for a sabbatical. How come, I asked myself, some people have so much time and others very little? Why are some able to blissfully concentrate on doing one thing at a time, while others have to juggle a multitude of tasks, constantly on the verge of utter exhaustion? It is fairly obvious that what I had in mind in any case was above all myself.

Even though this had not originally been part of my plan, I soon settled to seriously study social time. The renowned anthropologist Edmund Leach was then Provost of my host institution in Cambridge, King's College. He was thoroughly familiar with a wide range of different conceptions of time embraced by indigenous people in the most remote parts of the world, who were thus bringing human existence into harmony with the universe, nature and their specific social order. We talked about the meaning of cyclical time and about the transformation myths of tribes in New Guinea. We even moved into linguistic territory, discussing, for example, the way verbs were being displaced by nouns, a phenomenon that can be observed in Western societies. Leach most generously invited me to use his own private library. Thus, I immersed myself into reading anything I could lay my hands on that was related to time.

Soon I learned of the existence of the International Society for the Study of Time (ISST). This society was to hold its next conference in Japan in July that year. Then, as now, its members come from a wide range of academic disciplines—physics, linguistics, musicology, sociology, sinology, you name it. The great—and, indeed the only—topic they have in common is time, in all its fascinating interdisciplinary multitude. I decided to submit a paper and set off for Lake Yamanaka at the foot of Mt. Fuji. In keeping with my budget, I used the Trans-Siberian Railway and later an East German freighter that took passengers on board. I borrowed the captain's typewriter for a last round of revisions of my paper containing deliberations on the relationship between different structurations of time and time measurement (Nowotny 1975).

Time has stayed with me as a topic ever since. At the conference I quickly learned more about the different disciplinary approaches to time and encountered interesting people. More conferences were to follow as the years went by and at a later stage I was even elected president of the society. I remained in touch with the founder of ISST, J. T. Fraser, until he passed away. In the meantime, my academic career had progressed. My little daughter took pleasure in her mother's exotic interests. She asked me clever questions such as "What is time?" and "Is time everywhere the same?" And she was delighted when she discovered the ambiguity of the English phrase "What time is it?"

Two temporal islands, one month in 1987 and another in 1988, made it possible for me to write *Eigenzeit*. There was no hurry, no deadline to meet—indeed, there was not even a publisher. The book had all the time in the world to grow and to weave together scientific and personal threads of time.

A retrospective distance of three decades creates sufficient space and time to ask new questions. What is left of the late 1980s conception of *Eigenzeit*? Of the longing for the Now and the desire to have more time to oneself and at one's disposition? Which are the social and scientific-technological developments with their host of expectations, anxieties and projections of the future that have moved to the foreground today? How has the relationship between life time[1] and *Eigenzeit* changed? Does a political dimension concerned with issues of time and temporalities still exist today, which seemed so pressing then? How do power and time relate to each other at present?

In retrospect, it is above all the continuities that stand out, perhaps because they seem to verify the anticipatory analysis. This includes the phenomenon of acceleration, which I had seen as closely linked to the dynamic of scientific-technological development and its economic impact. In this vein, I had written: "While in the phase

---

1 "Life time" refers to the whole of one's temporal existence—how one lives one's life.

of industrialization it was above all the equation of time and money which resulted from the industrial capitalist logic of production and made time a scarce commodity, time is now being speeded up itself: it is becoming accelerated innovation" (Nowotny 1994).

Today, innovation is omnipresent. It is the determined and robust anticipation of the future by the present, supported by the co-production agreement that science and technology have entered into with a society that has eagerly concluded a pact with the new. Innovation is anchored in political rhetoric. It has become a key term denoting a bet that politicians are wagering on an increasingly fragile future, in the belief that they have discovered a fail-proof mechanism that will enable us to weather any crisis.

The acceleration of innovation has become a matter of ever-greater urgency. The problems created by the loss of jobs owing to the unstoppable advance of technological automation need to be solved —by more innovation. The solution seems to lie in incrementally greater doses of innovation, and it is indeed innovation that is being counted on to create new jobs and to open up new possibilities. The radical changes that computerization and digitalization have wrought over the last few decades in the economic, social and political fields demand additional radical measures. In practice, however, it looks more like stumbling into a future into which promises of innovation are interwoven in very uneven ways. In the end, innovation must somehow combine the old with the new in unforeseeable ways. Innovation consists above all in re-combination.

Having said this, it cannot be denied that the phenomenon of acceleration is one of the most far-reaching consequences of the changes brought about by science and technology. Once again, time seems to be out of joint. What is getting under the skin of so many people today is the speed at which modern life and their own lives are being played out.

Most of us feel alarmed by the dizzying speed at which the world is hurtling along, a speed that transcends by far our biological, cognitive, neural and mental capacities. The result is a deep-seated sense of unease and massive stress. This can be countered either by timid defensiveness or by the compensatory opposite, the decision to go with the flow, where the evanescent Now becomes the last straw to hold on to in a present that has lost orientation.

What becomes visible here is one of the many lines of conflict resulting from the collision of different temporal regimes. Acceleration, however, is not only triggered by technology's electronic speed. It radically surpasses all human capacities, so much so that attempts at adaptation are doomed to irrelevance. What is lacking are efficient time transformers, the institutional and social arrangements and rule systems that work towards the integration and assimilation of different temporal horizons, speeds and regimes.

It follows that it would be rash to simply equate the acceleration we experience with technological acceleration. Hartmut Rosa, in *Beschleunigung und Entfremdung*, quite rightly distinguishes between technological, social and cultural acceleration. In part these processes cause one another; in part they are mutually contradictory. Technological acceleration is visible and palpable for all; it can be measured and is easy to pin down. Social acceleration makes the changes visible that take place in a society. It is often twinned with a loss of stability on the part of institutions, and building new ones takes time. The third characteristic is cultural acceleration, which is reflected in our awareness of the rapid pace at which we are living our lives (Rosa 2013).

Yet another recent book deals with the paradox of how time pressure continues to build despite efforts of using time-saving technologies. Its topic is the interlinkage between technological, social and cultural acceleration. Technologies are supposed to make life easier by streamlining processes and boosting efficiency. However, rather than becoming more plentiful, time is being compressed and becomes ever scarcer instead. In *Pressed for Time* (2015), Judy Wajcman identifies digital capitalism as the root cause of the increase in acceleration. She makes it quite clear that the process of technological innovation always offers a plurality of options. She adduces a wealth of examples to show the different uses people make of digital technologies. The processes by which we construct social reality with the help of digital technologies have not run their course for some time to come (Wajcman 2015).

I fully agree with the diagnosis that the acceleration we experience is not the direct result of the technologies whose working speeds are so radically different from ours. But when I speak about the dynamic of accelerated innovation, it is not only these technologies I have in mind. That dynamic is generated through the multiplicity of social interactions that are built into, facilitated and mediated by the technologically new production processes and products. Their effect is to be found in the networks that are both socially condensed and geographically expanded. They contribute to the interactive game by creating ever-changing social and economic expectations. This gives rise to the temporal complexity which overwhelms us (Nowotny 1998).

The linear sequence of working steps and procedures has been replaced by the omnipresent expectation of the capability to master simultaneity. Prompt execution in real time is taken for granted. As an organizational principle, "just in time" is being superseded by Industry 4.0, which is currently spreading to more and wider areas. Work and everyday life are being shaped by project-like demands. The organizational preconditions for this stem from the potential for recombination, which in turn builds on the fact that many more and diverse interfaces are available. This is the environment that is indispensable for the temporal and spatial flexibility demanded by markets in the production of goods and services as well as in the workplace. Simultaneity seems to pervade everything.

Seen from this perspective, the experience of acceleration results from the multiplication of expectations that we want to—and presumably have to—meet. It is therefore not the technologically enabled greater speed as such that troubles us. The acceleration we experience is a consequence of the complexity arising from the dense economic and social interconnections as parts of a system that is enabled, boosted and expanded by technology.

This also applies to the acceleration of natural growth processes that Bernd Scherer has highlighted. Biotechnological regimes are superior to traditional breeding methods to an extent that was unimaginable in the past. In increasingly sophisticated ways, nature is being duped into stepping up its pace. In a convergent development, new financial and business models are created to open up new markets for products maturing ever more quickly. Even the obsolescence traditionally built into industrial production is becoming outdated. It is automated (Scherer 2016).

What these trends might mean in the future for that only true and rare resource, time has been outlined by Jacques Attali (2006) in a dystopian vision of the 21st century. As it takes increasingly less time to produce and to market goods, time use shifts from production to consumption. We become the time slaves of consumer goods and services. We have to allocate time to make use of what we are being offered—be it transport, communication, entertainment or the access to information, which needs to be downloaded and integrated. Does this sound familiar?

Making a selection from this glut becomes more and more time consuming. Only slowly do people begin to realize that they will never have as much time at their disposal as they would need to learn all that is required of them to remain "employable." The markets react to this situation by offering material and virtual goods whose use is ever more time consuming. Part of the deal is the illusion that the time will come when these commodities will stand us in good stead — as if death could be postponed by activities that are as time consuming as possible. In the end everyone will realize that time is the only true and rare resource: no one can produce it, no one can sell it and no one can store it.

This ushers in the rule of the "hyper markets." States are replaced by markets and disappear completely. In a countermove to the rise in life expectancy, growth processes are shortened. Babies are born earlier; children learn to speak more than one language at an earlier stage and more quickly. All vital functions are speeded up and cut back — sleeping, making love, eating, learning, playing, making decisions. The great crisis, which in Attali's view is already upon us, is about to kick in. And in the far distance beckons the utopia of a "hyper democracy" (Attali 2006–2007).

The experience of acceleration as a key component of modernity and its metamorphoses are going to be with us for a very long time. What is striking about this foray into the recent literature is the fact that one phenomenon is consistently sidelined that I would highlight and prioritize in *Eigenzeit. Revisited*: the accelerating destruction of our natural environment.

From the felling of tropical rain forests to the loss of biodiversity; from the increase in catastrophic droughts to extreme meteorological situations also in our latitudes; from increasingly scarce water resources and the problems of the insufficient supply of foodstuffs to the challenges posed by the rapid spread of mega cities—all these phenomena adhere to a logic of acceleration that has set humanity on a seemingly irrevocable collision course with its inherited natural environment. While granting that nature has been subjected to processes of change by *homo faber* from the very beginnings, it is only now that human intervention has reached a scale where it jeopardizes the very survival of the human species.

Time is running out: will we succeed in a race against time to ward off imminent collapse? Open up sufficiently productive sources of renewable energy in due time? Supply sufficient quantities of water and food for a world population growing faster than expected? And will it be possible for science and technology to speed up the pace of cultural evolution so that life on earth remains worth living—or will this lead to side effects resulting in even more destruction?

Unlike nature's biological evolution that unfolds in a long-term perspective and has almost infinite timespans for trial and error, cultural evolution progresses with accelerating pace. Above all, we are the ones that produce the required variation and act upon the selection. We are the ones that cause the cultural equivalent of biological mutations. These are largely not left to chance but are the direct effect our interventions. But what do we know about the unintended consequences of human action?

It is no longer only the familiar time scale of human history that will decide this race. We are up against time scales of radically different orders of magnitude. This is the first major revision that I would like to introduce in *Eigenzeit. Revisited.*

A second revision is at least as significant and momentous. It is the acceleration of the multiplication of available data and, even more importantly, the growth of the capacity to store data, to process them and to make them available for multiple and different uses. Today's world is shaped by *Big Data.*

Digitalization and computerization have created global networks that are being used by states and their secret services, by the financial world, by criminals, by science and industry—by all of us. What makes this possible is algorithms. These are mathematically formulated procedures for the solution of specific problems in the form of highly sophisticated computer programs. They are the *dei in machina*, invisible and therefore all the more efficient. Algorithms are the soft underbelly of complexity.

The speed with which data are processed and recombined exceeds by far the capacity of human perception. All we can do is register their effect. What bothers the average user is less the speed than the fact that all data, once they have been gathered, entered and stored, can be called up at any time and put to new uses.

Storage is almost for eternity—or for that portion of eternity that will be left to us. *Privacy* increasingly turns out to be an illusion. And while legal battles are being fought over the "right to be forgotten" on the internet, the feats that the latest information and communications technologies are capable of and what we allow them to do with us have a profound impact on our experience of time. This leads to the next question: how have our perception and our experience of time been altered? What has become of our longing for the now?

Global simultaneity that is experienced in concrete terms and its economic and technological impact that I described in *Eigenzeit* have expanded even further in the meantime. "Whoever governs simultaneity controls the temporal dependenc[i]es derivable from it. Yet despite the attainment of ever higher speeds in the networking of information technology, despite the continuing expansion of the technological infrastructure which installs simultaneity, it remains an illusion" (Nowotny 1994).

The illusion resides in the assumption that technological simultaneity will do away with global inequalities. Even though it has been possible to lift millions of people around the globe out of the worst poverty, there are still countries where the number of mobile phones exceeds that of basic sanitary installations. The epidemic caused by the Ebola virus would have run its course with a far less dreadful toll in human lives if Africa's health care system had a sound infrastructure. And Europe is currently experiencing the confrontation with refugee flows that are no less than the desperate expression of the non-simultaneity of human existence.

This is the great temporal contradiction we live in. Technologically induced simultaneity leads to a homogenization of the perception of time while social asynchrony is growing in proportion to the gap created by inequality.

Participation in global communication demands both a standardized and an individualized experience of time. This is a precondition for synchronisation. Time is split into small, standardized units to be replicated and individually reassembled at will. The result is a short-term perspective that guarantees flexibility. It sets the key for the exchange of information as the primary mode of communication.

But what information are we talking about? And what is it about? In the age of Big Data the concept of information has been considerably broadened. Anything that can be processed as data becomes information. Big Data penetrates into countless aspects of the workplace and of everyday life. It evaporates the boundaries between private and public, between what is classified and what is released for public consumption. It creates links between the most diverse areas where human activity and the events resulting from it leave traces.

Data are indifferent. They are without meaning. It makes no difference whether the content they refer to is trivial or of geopolitical urgency. This is because all traces that can be turned into data are apt to answer questions they were rarely meant for. Claude Shannon, to whom we owe the theory of the transmission of information, was the first to point out that the content of transmissions was irrelevant to the act of transmission. His definition of information counts only the number of bits required for the transmission of the system's state.

So what does Big Data do to time and our sense of time? It operates in the temporal regime of electronic data processing, which is not directly accessible for our temporal perception, biologically limited as it is. But being part of globally operating electronic networks enables it to absorb all the traces we leave, provided they can be transformed into data. The traces are many. They include the minutest trivia of everyday life: the countless social interactions that connect us with our fellow human beings on a daily basis; the traces left by our reading and listening habits; our consumer behavior; the number of steps we have taken and our changes of location plus whatever means of transport we have made use of. And so on and so forth.

What do we receive from Big Data in return? Targeted information, customized to our individual profile. What kind of information? Information about anything and nothing in particular. About things that are supposedly good for us and that we should therefore be doing. We even pay for this information while we supply the required data for free. What we receive in return is a multifaceted offer, a glut of options: purchase this book, that gadget, those designer shoes. This is where you want to go for your next holiday. Do this for the sake of your health and if you do sports, do exactly that which will improve your performance.

Big Data record the past indiscriminately. The more traces, the more data and, therefore, the better. Content does not matter. Questions concerning the *Why?*, the motivation, are replaced by questions of *What*. Only *What* questions generate data that are fit to be used over and over again—for other purposes, other questions, in other contexts. This transforms meaningless data into something that has meaning and significance. Predictive analytics is all about enabling predictions of our behavior in the present and in the immediate future, based on our behavior in the past—in other words, on the traces we have left.

Big Data homogenizes the past. Since all data are in principle fit to be used for purposes as yet unknown, the past is deprived of depth of focus. It becomes an abstract segment of time, a t_1, located on an equally abstract timeline. A discrete event becomes a *data point*, one among millions.

Connections established by algorithms make the relationship between patterns of behavior in the past and in the future. The information supplied to us by the commercial operators of the big-data networks contains a personalized promise for the future to be redeemed as soon as possible. Given this deluge of information, it is little wonder that news items, messages, instructions and promises vie desperately for our attention all the time.

Attention, as has often been noted, has become an economically scarce resource. The big internet corporations in charge of the data networks are ingenious in turning this scarce resource into as much profit as possible.

As users, we find ourselves confronted with the question of whom or what we should lend—or sell—our attention to. This reawakens the longing for the now in a new, unexpected manner in the midst of everyday life saturated with information and communications technologies. For some the solution lies in mindfulness, in focusing consciously on oneself, on breathing, on one's thoughts—or the absence of thought. Mindfulness is consciousness that is purposefully directed at the present, at the here and now; at calling for a break in the routine of living; at interrupting the familiar way in which time passes; at immersing oneself for a short time as a different way of experiencing time.

This is one more reason why music lets us enter into a different time frame. Music presupposes mindfulness. It is full of intervals and pauses. In some pieces by Johann Sebastian Bach, the interval is longer than the note that precedes it. Longing for the moment, however, is not to be satisfied only by engaging in mindfulness or listening to Bach sonatas. It is too deeply inscribed in our existence. Inexorably, the biological arrow of time points forward. Mindfulness would like to wrest moments from it that are not subservient to its time regime, notwithstanding the certainty that time's arrow will ultimately overtake all moments.

As so often in the history of humanity, technology intervenes. It alters not only our relationship with the environment and our fellow human beings but also with ourselves. It alters our experience of *Eigenzeit*. The endless multiplication of the amount of electronic data and the increasing density of the networks create a new, technology-based set of options to satisfy the longing for the moment: medial *Eigenzeit*.

The technological building blocks reside in the countless apps, programmed by the algorithms that underpin the connections from which the medial *Eigenzeit* flows. It is both standardized and personalized. The offers it makes are preselected and filtered—they are customized—for you, your lifestyle and your preferences. Medial *Eigenzeit* is accessible from everywhere via an iPhone or smartphone. It is ubiquitous and it manages both, to be available individually for each of us and to connect us to others. This is what makes it so attractive.

It seems that what I wrote in the last chapter of my book almost thirty years ago has come true in a completely unexpected manner. The longing for the moment, the longing to have time at one's disposal to be used at one's discretion finds its technological fulfilment. Medial *Eigenzeit* is available at any time. A digital switch, a key with an on/

off option is all that is needed. We are in full control of the moment, knowing that the next one can be switched on at any time.

Immersing oneself in medial *Eigenzeit* grants time to indulge in exchange with others. Rather than the conscious void that is being sought in the practice of mindfulness, it is time that is full of information — about the world, about friends, even if these are "friends" only in the social media sense; information about oneself and those parts of it that we want to share with others. It gives us a sense that we are incessantly engaged in communication with the entire world.

Medial *Eigenzeit* is time one has to oneself in order to spend it with those who are absent. It spells the end of boredom, that feeling that time is dragging on, that nothing of interest is even remotely in sight. For centuries people have sought refuge from boredom in distraction. Now distraction, entertainment and the conviction that all the latest developments are within easy reach are built into those small devices that channel medial *Eigenzeit* into one's fingertips.

What does the disappearance of boredom mean for the development of children? Who does not remember from their childhood those episodes of indefinably empty stretches of time that seemed unending? They generated a restlessness that became the breeding ground of ideas and of determined efforts to engage with something new. Can one really grow up—in any meaningful sense of the phrase—without ever having experienced bouts of boredom?

Sherry Turkle has conducted in-depth interviews with American youngsters and with managers of hi-tech companies. These interviews permit insights into a world where all that matters is *instant* communication on a broad front. The youngsters practice what Turkle has called "continuous partial attention." The capacity for conversation and the command of body language are being lost. This new generation has problems listening to others and developing empathy. Turkle, however, does not consider conversation a lost cause yet. We should treat communicative behavior as we treat eating—to be conducted with a set of rules and in moderation (Turkle 2015).

Rules have to be formulated by someone and their observance requires self-discipline. Here, too, medial *Eigenzeit* promises relief. It supplies us with direct information about our behavior in ways not previously available.

Countless apps now offer observation of the self in real time. Biomarkers—measurable indicators of vital signs and various bodily states—are compared with standard parameters and/or yesterday's measurements. One can enter performance goals for the self that one would like to be tomorrow. Medial *Eigenzeit* can be further expanded with the help of newly available wearable electronics, textile garments with integrated electronic devices. The aim is to monitor around the clock the functions of the entire body.

Biomarkers are "selfies" shot by our vital functions. They make the bio-temporal fluctuations of our inner rhythms visible. This data, too, is passed on continuously to be combined with other data for ever new purposes. Each individual is both connected in collective real time to countless others and simultaneously singled out as a unique human being. Uniqueness only makes sense if there is a frame of reference composed of the uniqueness of the others. The self feeds its data into the collective in order to be confirmed as self by the collective. This is yet another self-referential loop inherent to and enabled by medial *Eigenzeit*.

It is also one of the reasons why medial *Eigenzeit* fits seamlessly into the "sharing economy" and merges easily with what has been termed "open innovation." This creates an all-round win-win situation: the big internet corporations are tremendously profitable; small start-ups are encouraged to put their latest apps on the market and not to be deterred by the probability of failure. Even users stand to benefit.

One of the benefits that should not be underestimated is the consolation medial *Eigenzeit* extends to those in need. Whenever one is overcome by the anxiety of continued acceleration, of things spinning out of control and by the realization that one may not be able to achieve the goals set for oneself, the communicative gift of the moment is on offer: you are not alone to be plagued by these anxieties.

But even though medial *Eigenzeit* continues to proliferate in our lives in countless variations, it is limited in duration. Even if it devours the greater part of the day—there is more to everyday life than medial *Eigenzeit*. Unexpected things happen. The vicissitudes of life are unconcerned with temporal arrangements. And time's arrow points steadily forward, unimpressed by anything else.

The moments we spend with *Eigenzeit*, whether in its virtual or its real variant, are part of life time. *Eigenzeit* and life time are bound together in a mutual entanglement, marked by a productive tension that defies resolution. Given the finitude of one's life time with its unknown expiration date, the yearning for the present moment and the wish to have time for oneself expresses our deeply conflicted longing for the duration of human existence.

This tension is the product of life time's harsh and undeniable facts and the wish to make endurable what makes life worth living. *Eigenzeit* is set to mediate—between growth and decay, between disease and death on one hand and *joie de vivre* on the other. It grants us temporary unity with the self while always remaining precarious. Such unity must always be wrested from life time and requires constant reintegration.

Only at first sight does this seem not to apply to medial *Eigenzeit*, given its tendency to shy away from tensed states with the help of "instant" communication. In vain. The self is constantly being reconstituted medially by social interaction. Its identity consists in a multiform, variable entity, but there is no escape from the limitation imposed by a finite life time. Yet the constantly recurring constitution of the medial self opens up a new level of self-reflection. The self is in a position to observe itself and to intervene. It can share with others its changing embedding into its life time.

An overdose of medial *Eigenzeit* leads into the blind alley of egotism where people no longer can reach out beyond themselves and lose the capacity for empathy. "Friendships" that hardly scratch the surface cannot conceal the fact that the self may be hollowed out. Life time loses its resilience. Reflecting on the tension between medial *Eigenzeit* and life time may, however, also lead to the emergence of new forms of solidarity. It can make people connect with others, provided their self is open for others and ready for forms of cooperation that cannot yet be envisaged.

However imaginative and creative the individual strategies may be that link *Eigenzeit* and life time, they prove insufficient when confronted with the time scale of institutions or societies. It suffices to point to the acceleration of the human destruction of the natural environment to realize how difficult it is to fit the human lifespan into larger time scales.

How well equipped are current institutions to oppose the growing time pressure and the expectation of people's constant accessibility? What is their contribution to making the tension between life time and *Eigenzeit* productive? Institutions are time transformers. In principle, they command all the resources and the legitimacy required to coordinate, balance and adapt the temporal horizons and regimes of all parties concerned. What is lacking today, however, is institutional spaces, free to experiment with new ideas. Institutions lack the courage to experiment with different temporalities.

No time is set aside by institutions for reflection on these dilemmas or for institutional self-reflection. The institutions we have today were created as frameworks of reference and as means of regulation for the problems of the past. Their capacity for providing the kind of "temporal governance" required today is woefully underdeveloped. First, the long-term perspective is missing. Second, they lack what it would take to counter the neoliberal pressure for improvements in efficiency. This applies to many of our contemporary problems, from climate change to the threat that automation poses to the labor market.

In 1930, the renowned economist John Maynard Keynes gave a lecture at the students' club of the University of Madrid in which he shared his thoughts about the prospective economic future awaiting the generation of his grandchildren. Most of these predictions made for a time span of 100 years regarding economic growth and affluence have come true in the meantime. One prediction, however, baffles us today: Keynes prognosticated that the average working day in 2030 would only last three hours.

Meanwhile, automation is progressing rapidly. Machines are learning to do what human beings do and are getting better at it all the time. It hardly needs saying that they take infinitely less time and soon will be encroaching on middle-class jobs. It is not 2030 yet, but the urgent questions concerning the societal reallocation of work and the separation of work and income remain unresolved.

In retrospect, it seems that the politics of time, understood here as the search for an alternative distribution of work and leisure, has lost its relevance. The considerations I put forward in *Eigenzei*t were based on a broad political articulation. It included the demands of workers for greater time sovereignty, socio-political arguments in favor of a work-life balance and a more just distribution of paid and unpaid work between women and men.

Today the demand for more jobs, regardless of their quality, dominates politics. Consumer leisure time is on the increase in proportion to the growing online availability of consumer goods and services. Working hours have become more variable and more flexible. Largely unpaid time in care work is increasingly exposed to rationalization pressure, and relief is being promised by ever new time-saving technologies. Was the political debate of thirty years ago merely a u-chronia, a “no-time”? And what changes have reshaped the relationship between power and time?

A subtle distinction enjoyed in the past by those in power was the license to keep others waiting. Today, power manifests itself in the license to make others work hard to survive in the highly competitive atmosphere of technological acceleration and in the creation of new markets. Power is in the hands of those who succeed in transforming their temporal-economic competitive advantage into protected monopolies and oligopolies. Power manifests itself by skillfully expanding successful products and designs to new areas. One example is Apple transforming the mobile phone into an all-purpose computer. The corporation succeeded in creating a completely new entertainment system and to invent a new kind of shopping mall. Even though we are continuously told that “disruptive” technologies will wipe out all competitors, the tenacity of those in power to cling on to it is remarkable.

One of the central theses of *Eigenzeit* concerned the dissolution of the demarcation line between “present” and “future” as categories. A present predicated on—even obsessed by—innovation in science and technology and by innovation for its own sake appropriates the future. The present is turned into an arena for the deployment of knowledge and a wide range of activities are put into place to select and pre-filter the countless development options offered by the overwhelming potential of the technosciences. To safeguard evolutionary selection, a radical reduction must take place that pares them down to a few. This results also in an alteration of the quality of time.

The time paths of processes leading into the future thus become more stable and increase in density. Temporal dependencies are constituted. "The extended present has chosen the future and not vice versa" (Nowotny 1994).

With the end of modernity's belief in linear progress, the category of the "future" as a clearly envisaged goal has lost a great deal of its attraction. Today the future seems more fragile than ever before. The loss of the great historical horizon and the sole dominance of the West have fragmented it even more. The categories past, present and future do not have universal validity. Today they are undergoing another shift. The future is appropriated by the extended present. The intensity with which the future is evoked and the countless predictions that are being made are but steps in the process of its appropriation.

William Gibson, a well-known sci-fi author, once noted laconically: "The future has arrived—it's just not evenly distributed" (Gibson 2003). The future does not disappear, but its status has changed. Moving it nearer to the present has rendered its inherent uncertainties more clearly visible. Temporal complexity is generated through the unpredictable combination of the different components of the system, the different time scales involved and the different speeds at which they operate. Its dynamic is difficult to predict. Again, we are being made drastically aware of how limited our capacity is to foresee—let alone control—the unintended consequences of human action.

An extended present has particular repercussions on the temporal experience of the past. Some of the resources provided by that experience are lost, while new ones are gained. The past shrinks—it is levelled and appended to the present, a process largely affected by science and technology. The digitalization of past events opens up spectacular didactic opportunities and a new approach to these events. Visitors of Pompeii, Stonehenge, Laas Geel and other sites of antiquity can log in digitally at these sites, which allows them to follow the day-to-day lives of their former inhabitants and to take part in their (reconstructed) rituals without ever actually having set foot there.

The more the form of the representation and of its interpretation assimilates what is familiar and therefore contemporary, the more the distinctions vanish. The past stops being a "foreign country" in which "they do things differently" (as has famously been said), with alien structures and alien sensibilities. One of the most valuable resources of the past is in danger of being lost here: *the knowledge that it could have been different.*

This is compensated by gains. The more our own past, shaped by human history, is rendered present, the more the distant past is made visible with scientific precision. Not only do we look further back into the past, we also see more.

The knowledge generated by paleogenomics and the methods at its disposal today are completely rewriting the evolutionary history of our species as we know it. New relationships between us and the Neanderthals and Denisovans have been discovered. We learn that the regions of today's Amazon basin were probably first settled by populations that had made their way there from the Australian archipelago at a time when the distances were much shorter and the sea level much lower. We thus become aware of long periods of time, encompassing thousands of years, as though they were yesterday.

To an even greater extent, this is true of space, which has also become part of the extended present. The impressive pictures of Pluto relayed back to earth in July 2015 familiarize us with an extra-terrestrial object in the further reaches of the solar system as if it were as close to the earth as the moon.

Space is increasingly emerging as the vanishing point, where the past of the entire universe encounters the immediate future of humanity in an extended present. Behind us are the futuristic visions of the 1950s, the flying cars and other fanciful prognoses. Instead, we have driverless cars and drones, whose proliferation is imminent as soon as the markets are ready. Robotics has made huge advances. The progress artificial intelligence is making has begun to cause concerns even for the pioneers intimately involved in their development. Some assume that these rapid scientific / technological developments will result in the total loss of the future.

This is a view I definitely do not share. We live in an extended present that has appropriated many of the possibilities that we used to think of as located in the distant future. It brings us closer to the time scales of the universe and of evolution that exist independently of human activities but are made accessible through human activities. The epoch of the Anthropocene, marked by the undeniable impact of human intervention on the natural environment forces us into a cognitive and emotional confrontation we can no longer escape.

Arjun Appadurai has called the future a "cultural fact." He reminds us of the millions of people in India who, for the first time ever, are able to articulate their wishes and longings. Finally, they succeeded to have the "capacity to aspire" (Appadurai 2004). Perhaps this applies to us in the saturated West as well.

Our ideas of what a "good" society might look like are in danger of becoming stunted by the deluge of new apps, gadgets and toys that indulge our predilection for technology. Do we have consensual answers to the question raised in antiquity about *eudaemonia*, the good life we are striving to achieve not only for ourselves but for the societies we live in?

Science and technology release their tremendous potential only in co-evolution with society. The technosphere, this assemblage of technologies and their economic, societal and cultural preconditions and dispositions, unfolds a power that transforms reality. It reduces the distance between present and future in an unprecedented way. The reason why we will not lose the future is simple: there is no predetermined future, only a future that is as radically open as it is inherently uncertain.

I have reached the end of revisiting *Eigenzeit*. It leads me to a new encounter—with the Cunning of Uncertainty (Nowotny 2015).

To be continued...

References

Appadurai, Arjun. "The Capacity to Aspire: Culture and the Terms of Recognition." In *Culture and Public Action*, edited by Vijayendra Rao and Michael Walton, 59–84. Palo Alto: Stanford University Press, 2004.

Attali, Jacques. *Une brève histoire de l'avenir.* Paris: Fayard, 2006–2007.

Gibson, William. "The Future is Already Here – It's Just Not Evenly Distributed" *The Economist*, December 4, 2003.

Nowotny, Helga. "Time Structuring and Time Measurement: On the Interrelation between Timekeepers and Social Time." In *The Study of Time* II, edited by J. T. Fraser and N. Lawrence, 325–342. Berlin: Springer Verlag, 1975.

———. *Time. The Modern and Postmodern Experience.* Cambridge: Polity Press, 1994.

———. "Times of Complexity." In *Time, Order, Chaos: The Study of Time IX*, edited by J. T. Fraser, M. P. Soulsby, & A. J. Argyros, 91–146. Madison, CT: International Universities Press, 1998.

———. *The Cunning of Uncertainty.* Cambridge: Polity Press, 2015.

———. *Life in the Digital Time Machine.* The Wittrock Lecture Book Series. No. II. Uppsala: Swedish Collegium for Advanced Study (SCAS), 2020.

Rosa, Hartmut. *Beschleunigung und Entfremdung–Entwurf einer kritischen Theorie spätmoderner Zeitlichkeit.* Berlin: Suhrkamp, 2013.

Scherer, Bernd. "Wider die Herrschaft des Augenblicks." In *Die Zeit der Algorithmen (100 Jahre Gegenwart)*, edited by Bernd Scherer. Berlin: Matthes & Seitz, 2016.

Turkle, Sherry. *Reclaiming Conversation: The Power to Talk in the Digital Age*. New York: Penguin Press, 2015.

Wajman, Judy. *Pressed for Time. The Acceleration of Life in Digital Capitalism*. Chicago: University of Chicago Press, 2015.

V.

The Illusion of Control: Living with Digital Others*

My book *In AI We Trust: Power, Illusion and Control of Predictive Algorithms* was published in 2021. This article is a synthesis of my observations and analysis of the latest developments of digital technologies. ChatGPT and the amazing feats of Large Language Models (LLMs), to generate texts, sounds and images, took the world by surprise. It brings with it new opportunities and raises new concerns. One, however, looms even larger: are humans still in control of the technologies they create? Or are we at risk to fall into the illusion of being in control? We transfer agency to AI systems that are designed to project the illusion of communicating with another human being. Or, given the enormous concentration of economic power in a handful of a few large international corporations and the difficulties governments experience in regulating AI, is control handed over to Big Tech?

---

* Originally published in Helga Nowotny, "The Illusion of Control: Living with Digital Others," *Global Perspectives* 5, no.1 (2024): 117336. https://doi.org/10.1525/gp.2024.117336.

I argue that technology is about control. It is designed to operate according to the functions and goals inscribed in it: we expect it to work! Control implies to foresee and prevent what can go wrong. Historically, the control of technology has been extended from guaranteeing the health and safety of workers to cover its growing impact on health and environment for all. The challenge facing the control of AI consists in extending control further to the impact it has on our mental and cognitive capabilities. Where there is control, there is also the illusion of control. Humans are always at risk of being overwhelmed by their senses and biases. Modernity has been full of hubris and excessive confidence in the power of technology, ignoring or defying its consequences. Generative AI, such as ChatGPT and its co-species, have exposed human vulnerability to anthropomorphism, which makes us see things, phenomena, and other entities as more human-like than they really are. Slowly, we learn how to live with the digital Others and how to keep from fooling ourselves. Regulation is urgently needed to control the concentration of economic power that has arisen. We must better understand how much control and of which kind we will need in a future that is shaped by the co-evolution between humans and the technologies created by them.

❐❑❐

Controlling Technology and Extending the Control over It

"On the highway towards Human-level AI, LLM are merely an off-ramp." This dismissive comment by Yann LeCun about Large Language models, which are the basis of generative AI such as ChatGPT, displays the confidence of someone who is a Turing Award winner now working for Meta as Chief Scientist in the fierce competition that has recently erupted between the major corporate players. Inadvertently, it summarizes the dilemma of control inherent in the development and deployment of any technology. We believe to know where the highway leads and that accidents will happen on the way. The metaphor promises speed, efficiency, and a clear sense of the destination. But to prevent accidents may require more than an off-ramp. During modernity, highways were built with ever more lanes, swallowing more land and land use, seemingly without end. Now, we build digital highways. The challenge inherent in any technology is how to retain control. I will argue that digital technologies require an extended definition of control and, given its cognitive and emotional impacts, special measures to guard against illusions of control.

The development of AI continues to be accompanied by techno-enthusiasm as well as by doubts and dystopian visions. Reaching Human-level AI may turn out not to be as straightforward as the construction of a highway. Whether the forthcoming technological advances are under control is an open question, both in the narrower techno-scientific sense but also regarding off-ramps and other safety features that need to be built into their design. The history of AI demonstrates that the pursuit of preset goals can be elusive. Initial attempts followed the use of logic and formal symbols which eventually led to an "AI winter," a dead-end that occurred before the advent of neural networks and the "unreasonable efficiency" of machine learning (ML) by letting algorithms (self-)train on an enormous amount of data. As for the inbuilt safety features: we are still trying to stem the tide of hate speech freely circulating through social media and to design algorithms that do not simply replicate and diffuse the discriminatory bias inherent in the data on which their predictions rest. Our credentials in dealing with criteria like trustworthiness, fairness, responsibility, transparency and others, are glaringly poor. Not to mention the impact on people's lives and jobs, on our understanding of the world and of ourselves. We rightly expect that the dominant technology of the 21st century, whose speed of development dwarfs everything we know from the past, somehow will be able to control the fallout.

Control of technology serves more than one function. It is an integral part of the design, construction, and operation to make technology "work." As a smooth and efficient functioning can never be taken for granted, control implies foreseeing and preventing what can go wrong. Errors are inbuilt, and accidents happen. The fault may lie in the design or lack of proper maintenance and repair. The interfaces between technology and humans are multiple and often unpredictable. Now we must add the impact on the natural environment as digital infrastructures need a lot of energy and depend on rare minerals often located in conflict zones.

Control is inherent to every technology, as otherwise it will not function. This includes the whole gamut of safety valves and other protective features. The problem is that we can never be sure whether these controls will be sufficient to ward off harm, prevent failure or developments in an undesirable direction. The processes underlying creeping errors remain invisible for a long time before they lead to collapse. As the effectiveness and the affordances of a technology increase, control expands as well. Beyond the immediate, technical functioning, it needs to account for what can go wrong, which increasingly encompasses the foreseeable, and possibly also the unforeseeable, consequences. Control must adapt in line with the dynamics of change it is expected to manage.

The road from controlling the technical functioning of the machine, making sure "it works," to the control over the effects it has on those serving it, the workers, and beyond, has been a long one. During industrialization and under pressure from the labor movement to which the dismal working conditions gave rise, the focus understandably shifted to the health and safety of workers. The profit of factory owners should not come at the expense of workers' lives and well-being. After many conflicts, workers' demands were heeded and their dire conditions improved. In many European countries, a state-sponsored welfare system was established with insurance and compensation for the millions of workers whose lives and health were at risk. Gradually, safety features became a central part of the extension of control, designed into the functioning of the machines and the environment in which they operated.

By now, at least in most highly industrialized countries, the increase of safety features in products and production processes, regulation, and standards has become the norm, and such features continue to proliferate. They extend beyond manufacturing and pervade market-approved consumption use. Backed by legislation and bureaucracy, certification of products and safety measures have become mandatory, enshrined in obligatory checklists, safety drills, extra protection gear, and risk-reducing infrastructures. Whether it relates to the safety of cars and traffic, keeping medication out of reach of children, or safeguarding nuclear power plants—control over industrial products and processes to guarantee their safety has become paramount. The approbation of new drugs and medical treatments takes years of randomized clinical trials to assure the public that harm is avoided and side effects will be known.

Thus, the control of technology has multiple, nested layers and continues to pervade our technological civilization. Control is expected to increase productivity and efficiency as well as guaranteed safety. Maintenance and repair, recycling, and disposal of waste have become indispensable for protecting the environment, with the ambitious goal of a circular economy on the horizon. But control also has a dark side. It exerts power by installing constraints on things and processes, while prescribing how to interact with them, which easily can transform into control over others and the rights they have. The widespread fear of digital surveillance and its abuse by governments is a forceful reminder of the power of control exerted through technology. It can be visible like the surveillance cameras in public places or more surreptitious by following our digital traces, legitimized as being "only" for our safety.

It is difficult to pinpoint the exact locus of control. Control has been installed by humans and the technological devices are operated and owned by humans, following their instructions and goals. The agents of control are the large corporations with their concentration of economic and political power. They are the State, represented by its institutions, but also each of us when we conduct our daily lives and relationships with each other. Control flows through the multiple links that constitute a socio-economic and technological system. It changes form and purpose, including the answer to the question: *quis custodiet ipsos custodes* (who oversees the overseers). Therefore, control *of* technology and *by* technology makes it difficult to install regimes of accountability and responsibility. For a long time, efficiency had absolute priority. We begin to realize only now that we will have to invest more into resilience.

Where there is control, there is also its shadow—the illusion of being in control. Humans were always at risk of being overwhelmed by their senses and biases; by the wish to believe what they wanted to believe, even when contrary facts stared into their face. The causes for such illusions are many. They range from the overconfidence that disproportionately affects political and economic leaders, to the gullibility reserved for simpler minds. Illusions are nurtured by the cognitive biases we all have, but individual biases are reinforced by social and economic circumstances, by information and misinformation, and by the institutions and cultures into which we are socialized. Illusions of being in control are put to the extreme test in war when both sides are convinced that each will win, with technology on their side.

One peculiar feature of the illusion of control is its blind spot. Those who are in its grip fail to notice their condition until a clash with reality forces them to do so. The history of humanity is full of stories of human hubris, of excessive self-confidence, originally in defiance of the gods and in modern times in defiance of the unintended consequences of human action. Technology makes it all the easier as it provides an intermediary shield, raising the question whether the digital technologies that invade our lives will enwrap us even more in the illusion of being in control. Or will they have the contrary effect—that they and the powers behind them will control us?

The Challenges of Controlling AI

When Blake Lemoine, a software engineer at Google, shortly after a limited version of LaMDA—a generative AI specializing in dialogue—had been opened to the public in August 2022, told the *Washington Post* that he became convinced that it is "sentient," he caused a stir.

Google was quick to dismiss him on grounds of having violated the company's confidence rules. His professional colleagues were more outspoken but equally swift in declaring that he was wrong. They were unanimous in proclaiming that no AI had attained (as yet) anything like being "sentient," let alone some form of "consciousness." The public was reassured that Artificial General Intelligence, AGI, although high on the research and innovation agenda, was far in the future, and so was "singularity," the point in time when machines would overtake human cognitive capabilities. Yet behind the scenes, the race between Google, Microsoft and a growing number of start-ups staffed by their former employees continued to take the convergence of ML and LLM a decisive step forward and to release a new generation of generative AI models to the public.

The incident of sacking Lemoine and the reasons behind it were soon overtaken by the excitement caused by the release of ChatGPT, the generative AI developed by OpenAI and financed by Microsoft. It rapidly turned mainstream, raising fears about students deploying it to write essays or what it would mean for journalists if articles can be written with amazing speed on almost any topic. Others worried that in 2026 LLM will run out of high-quality texts that are already publicly available on the Internet and that this might entail a downhill ride towards literary mediocracy (Andersen 2023). As a remedy, the generation of synthetic data is already underway. But the capabilities of Generative AI do not end there. In addition to writing almost any text, they produce images following the prompts of the user or compose music in whatever style wanted. The pecuniary consequences for artists are obvious and claims for their copyrights are already fought out in courts, as the lawsuits against Meta currently lodged in San Francisco show (e.g., the class action led by Chabon, Hwang, Klam et al.; *Kadrey, Silverman, Goldman vs. Meta Platforms*).

This is only the beginning. Google reacted by releasing its version, Bing, a dialogical generative AI that promptly upped the stakes of everything that can go wrong. More foreseeable und unforeseeable consequences are likely to follow with the rapid diffusion and adoption of these digital products soon to inundate the market. DeepMind plans to bring to the market a new generation of "PAs," Personalized Assistants, designed to guide you in your decisions and how to lead your life. Behind the excitement and bafflement, anxieties concerning the most fundamental questions about the relationship between humans and the technologies created by them return with insistent urgency: how can humans keep control of the machines they have created and how liable are they to fall into the illusion that from now on the bots, or those operating them, are in control?

The incident about the former software engineer at Google is a tale about the illusion of not being in control. An illusion is a cognitive state which is out of sync with reality. If we are in thrall with an illusion, we are convinced that what we see, hear, and believe accords with reality. Only after an imploding clash with reality does the beholder realize that it has been an illusion. In the case of Lemoine, his professional peers declared so on his behalf. Obviously, this raises questions about the role of scientific and professional expertise, underlining the necessity of a commonly accepted framework of reference. Once scientific authority is no longer accepted as the arbiter of a shared and commonly accepted reality, we risk falling into a state of anomie, consisting of "personalized realities" that obliterate common ground.

These tendencies manifest themselves in the free circulation of fake news and deliberate misinformation through social media, which has reached an unprecedented level and threatens to undermine our shared understanding of the world. Since the Enlightenment, the shared assumption is that science stands for an approximation of Truth. Science is "organized skepticism," which means that scientific claims are critically evaluated in accordance with specified rules for argumentation and empirical validation. In liberal democracies the regulative idea of Truth has served us well, but it remains to be seen how it can stand up when it is being delegitimized. Once an accepted frame of reference becomes eroded and replaced by a "Googled" or "felt" Truth or by the infamous "alternative facts," liberal democracies and the place of science are at risk.

The recent encounters with generative AI have also exposed our vulnerability to anthropomorphism, to seeing the systems in which they are embedded as more human-like than they really are. By becoming extremely adept in mimicking human language and other cognitive abilities, including scientific and artistic creativity, the line between the "natural" tendency to anthropomorphize as expressed in the language we use in our dealings with technology, and the belief that the technological artifact is indeed an entity that "knows," "understands" and "thinks" becomes ever thinner. The un-reflected use of such words, which are relatively harmless if they refer to familiar technologies that we have incorporated into our world and hence under control, can transform into a dangerously compelling illusion of being in the presence of a thinking creature like ourselves (Shanahan 2023).

This puts us closer to the moment that Alan Turing defined as the arrival of a genuine artificial intelligence, namely when it is impossible to distinguish whether one is speaking to a real person or being able to recognize the image of a real person compared to a composite artificial face. However, the rapid advances in facial recognition and language processing have led to dispute Turing's definition and even to declare it as obsolete. Everything we know about the construction and functioning of these artificial systems tells us that they are very different from human understanding and our mental and cognitive capabilities. Being led to believe that the bot is a human agent may therefore be more of a sign of human gullibility than a testimony of the presumed "intelligence" of the machine which, in any case, is not the same as human intelligence.

Despite the many caveats reminding us that generative AI are only mathematical models, our anthropomorphic tendencies have a profound effect on how we relate to them. They model the statistical distribution of tokens from the vast public corpus of human-generated texts that tell us what words are most likely to follow the sequence of words in the question we ask (Shanahan 2023). And yet, they continue to amaze us by their speed and versatility, being able to switch tone and genre in the answers they give according to our questions. We tend to be also more lenient in tolerating errors when committed by a machine compared to errors by humans when we believe it to be more "objective"—another bewildering inconsistency in how we learn to live with the digital Others that are so clever in imitating and pretending to be like us.

Control is about power and domination. The illusion of control confuses what or who exerts power over whom or what, and how it happens. The deep-seated propensity to anthropomorphize a technology by treating it as if it were a human is a confusion about agency, identities and relationships. From experience, we know that neither is unambiguous. They may change. Our perception and knowledge of the world we share with others and what we assume to be mutual understanding is continuously challenged and in need of being reconfirmed. We may also collude with the machine, despite knowing that doing so is not in our interest and may even harm us. This happens when we hand over data about the most intimate aspects of our lives to Big Tech in return for their convenient services. We are cognizant that algorithms have been designed to boost engagement and yet we remain in an addictive relationship. All addicts live in the illusion that they can exit at will. If we mistakenly believe the AI to be "human," we give up control over who we are.

The power of technology has permitted us to do things that otherwise would be unthinkable. It has enabled the human species to transcend some its biological limitations, and the temptations of further enhancement know no limits. At the same time, it has revealed our biological limitations and our deep and intricate interconnectedness with other living organisms and the natural world around and within us. The flip side is the power technology has over us. It forces us to behave in certain ways, from observing traffic lights to obeying when facing a gun. Erroneously, we think that technologies are neutral and autonomous. Yet, they all have goals designed into their functions. They follow instructions, sophisticated as they might be. Whether technology is used in ways that are beneficial or to suppress other human beings—it is never about technology alone. Human agents have transferred agency to the machines that carry out functions to attain precisely specified goals. Human agents have interests, be it profit or to advance scientific understanding. Nowhere are the effects more profound and transformative than in our dealings with AI.

The Enchanted Universe of Our Ancestors

We are thus facing a range of complexities that fail to be captured by superficial references to human-machine interaction or by well-intentioned attempts to create an ethical, responsible, fair, beneficial AI, aligned with human values. The efforts to transfer and incorporate such properties into digital machines are sometimes compared to the task of educating children. We want them to grow up and become responsible members of society. This is a laudable task, but it reinforces the goal to make the machines more human-like, not only in the level of their intelligence, but also in their moral and ethical principles. Before jumping to trans-humanistic and premature conclusions, it might be worthwhile to reflect on how to achieve a more profound cultural change, the practice of a digital humanism (Werthner et al. 2019).

Marshall Sahlins, a towering figure in cultural anthropology, has left a posthumously published tribute to a world he calls the Enchanted Universe (Sahlins 2022). "Most of Humanity" lived in a world surrounded by meta-persons or spiritual beings. These were gods of various standings, ancestors, souls of plants and animals, and others who were immanent in human existence and, for better and worse, determined human fate. They were not "outside," but together with human persons formed one big society of cosmic proportions. In this Enchanted Universe humans were in a dependent, but also in an interdependent position. The meta-human powers were present in every facet of human experience and in everything that humans did. They were the decisive agents in human existence and the undisputed sources of success, or lack of it; they were involved in hunting or political ambitions; in repairing a canoe or cultivating a garden; in giving birth or waging war. Interdependence was manifest in the continual ritual invocation of spirit-beings through numerous cultural practices. Everything was the material expression of their potency, and nothing could be undertaken without evoking the powers of the meta-humans.

A major transformation took place some 2,500 years ago, during what Karl Jaspers called the "Axial Age" (Joas and Bellah 2012). Timing, geographic reach and the concept itself continues to be controversially discussed, but there is agreement that the immanent social order of the Enchanted Universe dissolved and gave way to a transcendental superstructure. The immanentist assumption that the capacity to achieve any objective depends on the intervention and approval of supernatural forces was replaced by that of "another world." It is separate from humans, constituting its own reality outside and above them—a transcendental world which we recognize as the objective reality in which we live today. Researchers working with Sheshat, a large data set of prehistoric societies, detected a correlation in the rise of social complexity in early societies that coincides with what they call the advent of moralizing punishing gods (Turchin, forth coming). The transcendental realm is at the root of the monotheistic religions and the fundament of modern societies with the rise of differentiated spheres of "politics," "religion," "economy" and "science." It paved the way for modernity and the belief in the linearity of progress.

Seen through the transcendental lens, we "moderns" are convinced that our ancestors "only believed" in the Enchanted Universe, while "in reality" they "knew" better (Latour 1993). In other words, their Universe was a perpetual, collective illusion. Sahlins refutes this interpretation. "We share the same existential predicaments," he writes, "as those who solve the problem by knowing the world as so many powerful others of their kind, with whom they might negotiate their fate." The common predicament is human finitude. Just like our ancestors, we are not the authors of our life and death, as we depend on a world that is not of our making.

And yet, more and more *is* of our making, beginning with the enormous impact humans have on the natural environment during the short period now called the Anthropocene. The world we inhabit is ever more a human-made world, dramatically changed through human intervention. It is populated by sensors, satellites and space telescopes that bring information about what happened in the universe millions of years ago into the present. "Welcome to the mirror world" I wrote in my book, referring to the digital world in the making (Nowotny 2021). Tiny robots are used to deliver medicine into those body parts where they are most effective. We have begun to edit genes and to vaccinate tumor cells. With the help of AI, brain waves can be transferred to a computer that transforms them into speech. We continue to create numerous artificial entities, non-human digital Others, with whom we share power and with whom we negotiate to gain or retain control. We seem to have reached what Giambattista Vico adumbrated in his *New Science* (1711), namely that "*verum* (*the true*) and *factum* (*the made*) " are interchangeable—we only understand what we made. The true and the made are reciprocal, each entailing the other.

I am not suggesting that with the end of modernity, characterized as the Weberian disenchantment of the world, we are about to create a new, digital re-enchantment. The transhumanistic movement and long-termism[1] is in my view only another flight of fantasy and wishful thinking to escape human finitude and death. Yet, the transcendental bearings on which the modern world relies are undergoing a long-term process of erosion. Are we creating a supra-human force, this time in a secular vein, or are we challenged to find novel ways of living with the digital Others created by us? We do not fully understand Vico's *factum,* the machines we have created, neither in the details of how they work, let alone in the implications they exert on us, their

---

1 Long-termism is an aspect of "effective altruism," a philosophical and social movement that gives priority to improving the long-term future of humanity. Critics claim that by focusing predominantly on "existential risk," it favors eugenics and neglects today's foremost problems.

creators. We transfer agency to them when we begin to "believe" that everything predictive algorithms tell us must come true, forgetting about probabilities and that the data are extrapolations from the past. At the heart of our trust in AI lies a paradox: we leverage AI to increase our control over the future and uncertainty, while at the same time, the performativity of AI, the power it has to make us act in the ways it predicts, reduces our agency over the future (Nowotny 2021).

In the Enchanted Universe in which most of humanity lived, everything that was done happened with and through the meta-persons who decided the fate of humans. If we believe that predictive algorithms "know us better than we know ourselves" and that they "know" the future, do we not risk returning to a deterministic world view in which human destiny has been preset by some higher power? Most of humanity presumably experienced the enchanted world they lived in with a mixture of constant anxiety and awe, to which they responded with sacrifices and rituals. In contrast, our digital enchantment seems rather bland, although we are promised an ever more exciting and fulfilling virtual world. It is dominated by the monopolistic power of large international corporations that provide us with cheap entertainment and an overload of data that wants us to crave for more of what they offer to us. Although we partly see through these virtual illusions created by them, we remain under their spell.

Learning to Live with the Digital Others

The pandemic marked the recent clash with reality that shattered the illusion of many, including our governments, that we were as much in control as we had thought. Modernity generated hubris of all kinds, among those described in *Seeing Like a State* (Scott 1998). It boosted the conviction of being able to control everything — if not in the present, then in a brighter future to which the single-minded vision of linear progress, backed by planning and continuous economic growth, would lead. Today, the realization has set in that despite the many benefits modernization brought, it has also moved humanity closer to an environmental abyss and that the promises of a better life for all has failed many people. Inequalities have been on the rise within Western countries and the global North-South divide has hardly shrunk.

Our liberal capitalistic system has, as Martin Wolf poignantly writes, produced many angry people (Wolf 2023). Social media reinforce the already present tendencies of a further polarization in our societies, and emotions like anger and hate are easily captured by populists and nationalists for their purposes. We have gravely underestimated the role that imagination plays in politics and have failed to realize the extent to which any vision or ideal of a political regime, including liberal democracy, depends on imagination and the necessity of fiction (Ezrahi 2012).

Maybe the time has come to restore space for imagination as the positive side of illusion. If unchecked, both can run wild. The history of modern science is filled with attempts to reign in the imagination and to put the brakes of empirical verification on the senses and human passions. Objectivity in science is an ongoing story of keeping the temptations of an unrestrained imagination at bay while leaving space for it as a vital source of human creativity (Daston and Galison 2010). Imagination plays an important role not only in science and the arts, but also for the ways in which we conceptualize and perceive the future. As I have shown elsewhere, until a few decades ago the future was seen as a huge projection screen, filled with collective imaginairies. Some were dystopias, mirroring the grievances and fears people held at present. Others drew inspiration from science fiction and were filled with wondrous gadgets like flying cars or the amazing things computers would do. The future was seen as an exciting period ahead and, for the most part, it seemed desirable.

Today, this future has disappeared. As science fiction writer William Gibson wrote a long time ago: "The future has arrived; it is only unevenly distributed." It arrives with every new digital advance and does so more quickly and more overpoweringly than expected. As a result, the present becomes overloaded with data from the past and filled with data collected "live." The result is a continuous emotional and informational overload that fills every minute of the time we are awake and continues to monitor our physiological functions while asleep. We live in a present that has become densely compressed, as it has to absorb the digital future that continues to invade our lives (Nowotny 2020).

Digital devices have not, as promised, led to a decrease of our workload—on the contrary. We are too busy and captivated by downloading apps to have any time left to imagine a future that is rapidly dissolving in a digital haze. We are at risk of losing our capacity to imagine a desirable future, let alone the drive of wanting to shape it. Yet another illusion is lurking behind every "next gen" digital product —the illusion that we are not in control, infused with the belief that no alternatives exist to the advent of the Super Intelligence in the making. We are still in the grip of another modern dichotomy:—that there is either full control or none—and are in urgent need of will and the capability to imagine that it could be otherwise.

Yet, if there is any lesson to be drawn from the history of attempts to control the technology humans have created, it points in the opposite direction. Humans have held many illusions about the capabilities to control their aggrandized visions, only to be pushed back by the forces of Nature, which still holds the upper hand as signaled by the complexities of coping with climate change. Despite the sobering background of human hubris, including some of the most horrendous consequences of the illusion of being in control, we must avoid the illusion of having no control. Our ancestors from the Enchanted Universe would have told us that by practicing the proper rituals to invoke the goodwill of the spirits, they succeeded precisely because the power of the spirits had been transferred to them, empowering their activities.

Obviously, to gain control over the digital Others requires more than rituals and sacrifices. It begins with rethinking the concept of control and to reinvent forms of control that include care and responsibility. We have embarked on a co-evolutionary trajectory between humans and digital machines. If efficiency alone remains the overriding goal, we will be outpaced and overwhelmed by the machines very soon. If we pursue other goals, like building resilience into the system and how to innovate sustainably, the chances of keeping ahead are much greater. However, such goals must be embedded in the collective imagination, driven by the desire to reappropriate a future that is open, even if it remains uncertain. Embracing uncertainty will not restore us to being in control, but hopefully it will enable us to learn to live with the digital Others in a common world yet to be made.

References

Andersen, Ross. "What Happens When AI Has Read Everything?" *The Atlantic*, January 18, 2023.

Daston, Lorraine and Peter Galison. *Objectivity*. Princeton: Princeton University Press, 2010.

Ezrahi, Yaron. *Imagined Democracies. Necessary Political Fictions*. Cambridge: Cambridge University Press, 2012.

Joas, Hans and Robert Bellah. *The Axial Age and Its Consequences*. Cambridge, MA: Harvard University Press, 2012.

Latour, Bruno. *We Have Never Been Modern*. Cambridge, MA: Harvard University Press, 1993.

Nowotny, Helga. *Life in the Digital Time Machine*. The Wittrock Lecture Book Series. No. II. Uppsala: Swedish Collegium for Advanced Study (SCAS), 2020.

———. *In AI We Trust: Power, Illusion and Control of Predictive Algorithms*. Cambridge: Polity Press, 2021.

Sahlins, Marshall. *The New Science of the Enchanted Universe. An Anthropology of Most of Humanity*. Princeton: Princeton University Press, 2022.

Scott, James C. *Seeing Like a State: How Certain Schemes to Improve the Human Condition Have Failed*. New Haven: Yale University Press, 1998.

Shanahan, Murray. *Talking about Large Language Models*. Accessed January 25, 2023. https://arxiv.org/abs/2212.03551v4.

Turchin, Peter. "The Evolution of Moralizing Supernatural Punishment: Empirical Patterns." Forthcoming in *The Seshat History of Moralizing Religion*, edited by Larson et al. Chaplin, CT: Beresta Books.

Werthner, Hannes et al. "Manifesto on Digital Humanism." DIGHUM. Accessed June 20, 2019. https://dighum.ec.tuwien.ac.at/dighum-manifesto/.

Wolf, Martin. *The Crisis of Democratic Capitalism*. London: Penguin Books, 2023.

Future Needs Wisdom captures Helga Nowotny's critical spirit. In it, she looks back at her stellar career and recounts key experiences on the frontline of science and technology studies and across the global academic stage. This intellectual memoir reflects a life of world-class interdisciplinary research closely connected to the public sphere. As such, it provides an excellent introduction to her thinking, situating it in relation to major intellectual, political, and social movements of the time. Spanning her upbringing in Austria, doctoral studies in the American intellectual landscape of the early 1970s, life-changing sabbatical in Cambridge and rise to prominence at the University of Vienna through to her role in setting up the Collegium Budapest, trailblazing at ETH Zurich including her path-breaking book *Eigenzeit,* and her appointment as President of the European Research Council—these are all major moments of this fascinating life.

Nowotny achieves a double form of history-telling, a personal hybrid of life and intellect that shifts both backwards and forwards at the same time. *Future Needs Wisdom* is not really a memoir, nor is it an intellectual history, nor is it entirely a personal reflection or a summative philosophy. It is, in fact, all of these things fused together: her life, her scholarship, her thoughts, her triumphs, her misgivings, and above all her hopes and utopic aspirations. This work effortlessly spans the fields of science and technology studies, philosophy, sociology, feminist thought, political theory, complexity studies and information science.

Anthony Elliott

Distinguished Professor, University of South Australia

This is a fascinating memoir about an exemplary life. Exemplary because the encounters and accomplishments (as a scientist and as a leader of scientific institutions) have been so exceptional. Exemplary also because Helga Nowotny's story offers an example of a woman's path in science that will be inspiring inside and outside sociology.

Elena Esposito
Professor of Sociology, Universität Bielefeld

What an inspiring reflection on her intellectual life Helga Nowotny is gifting us with *Future Needs Wisdom*! I learned so much from reading this book written by a scholar known for her exceptional sharpness, insatiable curiosity, good judgment, foresight, and of course, wisdom! I urge researchers from across the disciplines to make time for this book, which imparts so many life lessons concerning the importance of uncertainty for creativity, the emotional life of research, and much more. Certainly, we will all be enriched by what we can learn from the author.

Michèle Lamont
Author of *How Professors Think* and
Professor of Sociology and
African and African American Studies, Harvard University

Helga Nowotny's academic trajectory has followed a decidedly non-linear and even unconventional path. She started in law, and then moved into sociology. But then feeling constrained by the limits of a single discipline, she embraced interdisciplinarity, striking out into the world of science and technology studies. This eclectic intellectual arc led her to help establish and ultimately become president of the European Research Council. Hers is an account of a remarkable life full of diversions and detours that has given her a polymathic outlook of great wisdom and insight into the big problems of the day.

Peter Ho

Senior Advisor, Centre for Strategic Futures and
former Head of Civil Service, Singapore